THE MAKING OF A PROPHET

Ron Rendleman

The Making Of A Prophet

Copyright © 2003 by Ron Rendleman

Published by Sterling Productions
P.O. Box 41
Sterling, Illinois 61081

All rights reserved. No part of this publication may be reproduced, stored in a retrieval system, or transmitted in any form or by any means, electronic, mechanical, photocopy, recording or otherwise, without the prior permission of the copyright owner.

Printed in the United States of America

ISBN 0-9650884-3-X

Other Books By Ron Rendleman

Tears For A King

Disciple In Blue Suede Shoes

You Can't Fly Home Again

Stepping Into The Supernatural

Red Sky

A Line In The Sand

Let The Games Begin

Cover Design: Jason Uriah White

Preface

You are about to embark on a rather unusual journey. The road you'll travel may be a little bumpy at times but in the end, I trust you won't regret undertaking it.

My motivation for this work is twofold: (1) to record for my family, and strangers alike, the many wonderful supernatural experiences I have had (I wish my granddad had written about his life). And (2) to give to those "who have eyes to see and ears to hear" information that will enable them to survive, physically and spiritually, the great tribulation about to come upon the world.

ONE

MY FIRST LESSONS IN SURVIVAL came as a teenager driving a cab nights in Chicago. To avoid getting held up after a couple of near misses, I learned how to size a fare up quickly before I let him in. I learned you never got involved in other people's problems no matter the circumstances. One night I dropped off a bunch of tanked-up businessmen at Soho's, a strip joint that paid me two bucks a head. I got the payoff from the club's doorman and headed my cab west. Three blocks up the street there was a Latino bar.

The first thing I remember was this well-built young Black staggering backwards out of the place with about eight Latinos after him. He got his back up against a light pole while they surrounded him on three sides. I didn't see any knives though Hispanics are big on that. No one spoke. They just waited, tensed like alley cats, for someone to commit himself. Passersby froze. I sat in my cab across the street with the engine running in case.

The Black was well-muscled and over six feet. He made the little men around him look like midgets. Slowly the circle closed. Abruptly the Black, while looking at the man to his right, hit the closest man to his left square in the mouth and the "whap" echoed across the street. The receiver of the punch flew through the air, bounced off a storefront and dropped to the sidewalk.

The Black put a couple of more out of commission until numbers overpowered him. Like wolves after a stallion they dragged him to the pavement. Never have I seen a man take such punishment. While four held him down, others took turns kicking his exposed stomach with pointed-toed boots. I thought to grab a jack handle from the trunk and help him, but I didn't. When they were done they calmly walked back into the saloon to celebrate the victory. The Black lay bleeding on the sidewalk and people stepped over him and continued on their way.

I drove away feeling guilty. I told myself I would have been a fool to get involved. I was out there to make a living, to survive in a jungle. Money was the life force of the jungle. I had to keep hustling to get my share and I had no time to worry about other people's problems. But the more money I made the more I wanted. I began doing stupid things like the night I picked up three swabbies (sailors) who wanted girls. I was still too green to have any contacts myself so I just drove down Clark Street to an old hotel, told them to ask for three fictitious names at the desk, took their ten dollars apiece and drove away, chuckling.

My joy didn't last long. When I pulled into the garage the boss said, "You have an appointment to see President Samuels tomorrow at 10 o'clock."

The CEO of Yellow Cab greeted me with, "So you're the one cheated three boys serving our country,

The Making Of A Prophet

huh? It was very clever, but it will cost your job plus the thirty you took them for." I went to work for Checker Cab the next week.

I liked the cab business in a way. It gave you real insight into human nature. Often the same businessman you'd pick up in the morning was totally changed when you got him that night with a few drinks in him. Most of the time he'd be hostile, ready to make someone else pay for the problems of his life. I realized before long why the old timers were so cynical--dealing with the public took all the nice guy out of you.

On my day off, which was always Monday, I would go out drinking with my friends and try to pick up girls. I remember one summer night we were walking down Randolph Street half drunk and this guy who was a head taller than I and better built was standing up against the front window of the Greyhound Bus station at Clark Street. Somehow I thought he looked like he needed an attitude adjustment. I began to egg him into a fight and he was about to oblige me. But before he ever got set, I slammed him two or three times with both fists and he hit the window hard and dropped. We ran to the car and scorched rubber before the "fuzz" showed. When I look back at my actions then, I know I was motivated by a drive, a frustration that made me drink and curse too much, pick fights, and generally take advantage of people to "get even." With whom was never clear but I'm sure my early upbringing played a large part.

I was born and raised in Chicago and my folks raised my younger sister, Jeannine, and me with a lot of discipline. My mother didn't know how to show love to us, and my father was too wrapped up in his own struggles of making a living to even begin to understand our needs.

Even as I write this I can still feel the ache of rejection, especially from my father. Raised on a farm, he had a lot of know-how concerning hard labor and why a motor wouldn't run. His corny jokes would drive my mother up a wall but send me and my sister into hysterics. I remember how desperately I would try to win his approval. Once in awhile he would throw me a bone--but there's little nourishment in a bone. One time when I was nineteen and newly married, I went over to his place to help him move a pile of dirt. We got into a minor disagreement and he angrily blurted out, "You're not half the man I raised you to be." For these many years those words still ring in my ears, and I'm sure they have been behind the force that drove me to prove to him and everyone else I could take on whatever the world had to offer.

Later in life when I began working with youth, I understood their hassles with fathers too tied up in business or hobbies and a mother always too busy with outside activities to give them the attention they needed to mature emotionally. I think this is why gangs have become so prevalent--the kids are starved for love and their peers answer that need.

Against my wishes, I got shipped off to a seminary to be a Catholic priest at the age of 13 and the following year to a military school in Onarga, Illinois. Razzings by upper classmen were common and I developed a hatred for rank and authority very early.

About the only thing that really held my interest was sports. I would get very excited when my family occasionally came down from Chicago to a football

The Making Of A Prophet

game or track meet. Mom would always say, "I don't care what you make of yourself, but be the best. If you want to be a garbage collector, fine, but be a good one!" I loved the physical contact in football, laying some guy out. Running the quarter mile in track was also a gas. I came pretty close to going to the state finals my senior year.

I went to Eastern State College in Charleston, Illinois, for a year, and that was the year I married a little saucy Italian named Gloria Gabriele. She was sitting in Chicago's Del's restaurant with her girlfriends when I happened to stop for a Coke after a hard day on a construction job. What struck me was her long dark hair and very pretty eyes--her likeness to movie star Joan Collins was remarkable. The same year I decided to attend Northwestern's Medill School of Journalism. That's when I started driving a cab nights.

By the time I was 25 we had five children: Nick, Vickie, Rita, Rhonda, and Roy and the rat race of making enough to support them wasn't fun. I'd gotten a job writing ad copy for Montgomery Ward, but in many ways advertising with its mind control techniques never appealed to me. I was ready for another challenge.

I'd lost weight dieting. A photographer friend took some pictures and encouraged me to go into modeling and TV commercial acting. Why not, I thought? If I didn't give it a shot, for the rest of my life I'd probably regret the decision. When I quit my advertising job, my peers couldn't understand how I could just pull out like that and take such a gamble. I detested their fears and the merry-go-round they couldn't seem to jump off of even though most of them wanted to.

Ron Rendleman

I began making good money modeling and doing television commercials and about a year later, I decided I could ride a horse at least as well as those dudes on TV. So I came home from work one day and said to my wife, "Hon, I'm going out to California and become a movie star." Her mouth dropped open. She didn't fight me but I could tell I didn't have her support.

However there was a slight problem--money. The trip and living expenses of at least a month would cost an easy two thousand. One night, sitting in a hot bath and sipping scotch, I got a great idea. A year earlier I had worked some as a printing salesman, calling on companies throughout Chicago, and I learned that since business was so competitive, printers were constantly looking for anyone who even looked like he might be able to sell for them. It was easy to get on a payroll.

Well, soon I was working for five of these printers at the same time without them suspecting I was drawing a salary from their competitors. It was a chore just checking into each place of employment every day. By the time I had hit the last, it was the middle of the afternoon.

It took two or three weeks for a printer to catch on, but by that time I would have another lined up and it certainly was an exciting life. Before long I had my little nest egg of two thousand saved up for my journey to the golden West. I justified my actions by telling myself that most printers were dishonest anyway and were engaged in payola with buyers.

I was in Hollywood only 24 hours when I found an agency willing to handle me, Goldstone Tobias. They sent me up to see Warner Brothers and Screen Gems

The Making Of A Prophet

and the psychology they used to get me the look-see was, "This man is acting in Chicago. He's out here on vacation and in two weeks returns to work. Are you interested in screen-testing him while he's here?"

Warner Brothers did and though an assistant director told me my test was excellent, they decided not to put me into their stable of 29 guys and pay me the $300 a week my agent was asking. I bummed around Hollywood till my money ran out; learned how the gigolos, the make-men, and other society dregs who feed off others survive, got fed up with the whole scene and drove back to Chicago to take up life with my family. The year was 1963 and President Kennedy had just been shot.

Somehow I had to find myself. I had no goal, nothing satisfied me. But it was good to be back with Gloria and the kids where I was once again king of my own domain. As I reminisce about those days, I know I tried to show our kids love and treat them equally. But to be really honest, my attitude on raising children was just like my dad's--they should be seen and not heard. Some people never learn. But I still say it is better to err in being too strict in raising kids than being too lenient.

When my income from modeling and acting began to dwindle some, I decided I ought to use my advertising experience to sell point-of-purchase displays. In April of 1966 I made a sales call on Don Baker, marketing manager of Scripture Press in Wheaton, Illinois. The thing I remember about Don was the softness in his eyes and his gentle manner. I was used to the cigar smoking, foul-mouthed promotion manager who gave you five minutes of his time if you could do something for him. Don began to talk to me about God and I thought he was crazy. He mentioned that he wasn't afraid to die because he knew God had forgiven him for his sins. That bugged me. How could he know that? I wasn't even sure there was a God. Where was God? Everything I did, I did for myself; everything I owned, I had earned (most of it). When I left his office I held three of his booklets and had a lot of questions that were to bug me for days.

One night I was lying in bed reading one of the books, *What's Life All About?* written by an evangelist, William Orr. I'd asked myself that a thousand times. The writer didn't put a story together with a bunch of Bible verses. He showed me the design of nature, of the universe, and said that design wasn't possible without a designer. That made sense. One particular example he used has stayed with me all these years. He asked, "Did you ever think how wonderfully designed you are? Take your nose, for example. By detecting odors it tells you where to find food or warns you of danger to help you survive. It starts the process of digestive juices flowing, it filters the air to your lungs, it points downward so you won't drown when it rains or blow your hat off when you sneeze." Perhaps it was a little silly, but it made perfect sense to me at the time. His final point was that God wanted man to love Him, but He would not force him to because then He would receive a robot-type love. That made sense too.

The weekend after finishing the book, I was fixing up a client with a prostitute. We were at a motel in Franklin Park outside Chicago and he was waiting to go upstairs and see the girl. While we were having a drink I happened to mention I had been out to Scripture

The Making Of A Prophet

Press and I remember him saying, "Watch out those people don't get to you."

"I think they already have," I answered. "I'm beginning to see some things I never saw before." He scoffed; he was more interested in the girl.

A few days later on Sunday, May 15, 1966, I was sitting in a Catholic church in West Chicago, the town we had recently moved near. I hadn't been to a church in years. We had kept the kids in a parochial school, hoping to give them a better education. My son, Nick, who was the oldest at 13, was serving mass as an altar boy. I was there because he needed a ride.

I began thinking about the book Don Baker had given me. According to the author, the emptiness I had felt inside for a long time was caused by my ignoring God. No matter how good life was--decent job, ego tripping before the cameras, or partying till dawn, the emptiness never went away. Like the song asked, "What's It All About, Alfie?" I mean how many times had I asked myself why was I on earth: to raise a family with an occasional outside laugh thrown in and that was it? Wasn't there any more to life than working to eat and waiting to die?

It was a six o'clock mass. There was a mere handful of old ladies in black shawls present in a church that was small and very old and dimly lit by candles. The young Franciscan priest began to pass out communion to the old ladies and announce fairly loudly, "The body of Christ," with each wafer. As I think back now, I still feel a rush of emotion as I remember those words. Those ladies were symbolically receiving what was missing in my life--Jesus Christ.

Tears began to flow as a great need to be loved

began welling up inside even as I was painfully aware that I was the last guy in the world to merit receiving any love. I knew how completely self serving my entire life had been; all the times I had been dishonest, morally corrupt, the hypocrisy, the pretense, the arrogance. I had little right to receive anything but heartache in return.

But even as I agonized, I became aware that there was a remedy. All I needed to do was reach out for it. However, I was being drawn into a dimension where I would not be in control and this was pretty scary. I remember I tried to make a deal on my terms: I would clean up my life, even start going to church in exchange for some peace. But I drew a blank. Some time elapsed as a battle raged inside me. Finally I knew what I would have to do. Bowing my head, with tears streaming, I breathed a deep sigh and... surrendered. Immediately, I began to get a wonderful feeling of love and joy and most importantly, forgiveness. I felt, magically, that I was being given a new start in life, that never again would I have to strive to receive approval from my dad or my fellow man. I had been unconditionally received by a heavenly Father.

After the mass ended I floated outside into the sunshine--that 60-pound sin monkey off my back forever. My boy looked at me quizzically, but if he noticed the tears drying on my face, he never said a word. As we drove home in silence I marveled at how differently I felt. Little did I realize I was about to embark on an incredible journey.

Ron and Gloria in Hollywood for Ron's screen test with Warner Brothers.

TWO

WHEN I ARRIVED HOME the first thing I did was awaken my wife. "Honey," I said, "something happened to me in church today. God has touched me, I know it. My life is never going to be the same."

She looked up at me from the bed and said, "It's about time." I asked her to join me in prayer, to seek God together right there.

She said, "Look, it's taken you 33 years to find God, don't expect me to find Him in ten minutes."

I understand now what a sudden shock it must have been for her. For years I wouldn't allow grace to be said at the table. I would not take my kids to church. If she went to church, I scoffed at her for wasting her time. I'd seen the big cars driven by the clergy and the way the poor were browbeaten into giving. What I didn't realize was that corruption is everywhere--even in religion, because man is imperfect.

I went to the priest, who was pastor of the church where God and touched me and told him of my experience. I needed to know more of what exactly had happened to me, but he didn't have any answers.

Subsequent experiences with men of the cloth, both Catholic and Protestant, have shown me that many clergy don't have a personal relationship with Jesus Christ. But there was one man who I was sure would know exactly what I had experienced--Don Baker, at Scripture Press.

Tuesday morning I was in Don Baker's office asking him a million questions. Of course, he was excited and very helpful and asked me to speak at Scripture Press's chapel service. A lump came to my throat; I had never addressed more than 15 people in my life. But two hundred? I fought the idea for some moments then told him I would because it was the least I could do to repay God for what He had done for me. After I finished speaking several employees had misty eyes when they came up to congratulate me.

My life began to change drastically. I started reading the Bible which really came alive for me and I learned why I had been so frustrated. All the parts of my life were like the broken spokes of a wheel, they weren't attached to the hub, just hanging loose. But now I had a hub--Jesus Christ.

I began to tell everyone I met about my wonderful experience, but it was pretty obvious most people weren't interested. So I backed off, or at least, thought I did, but I'm sure I antagonized some. Many claimed to be believers, and I couldn't figure out why their lives didn't reflect that.

My family was happy with the changes they saw. I was praying now at supper time and had more time for them. Within months all of them except the youngest, little six-year-old retarded Roy, found what their daddy had, and they began to go through hassles. Rhonda, for instance, would take Billy Graham tracts to her Catholic junior high school. I got called in by a very zealous

The Making Of A Prophet

Jesuit priest who told me that I was confusing my daughters and that I should let the school handle their religious instructions. I asked him if he ever had an experience with Christ. Evasively, he said, "Oh, I met young men at Loyola, where I used to teach, who got emotional. It's just a phase you're going through, you'll get over it." I thought to myself, *another one with head knowledge, but no heart knowledge.*

Nick was attending St. Francis High School in Wheaton. He would come home and tell me that the religion teacher, Brother Luke, was teaching that the miracles in the Old Testament didn't really happen the way the Bible said they did. So I asked him to set up an appointment with the Brother some evening. I asked Lud Golz, a pastor of an independent Bible church I had started attending to go with me.

After the small talk was out of the way, I asked, "Brother Luke, concerning the miracles in the Bible, where do you draw the line? What part do you accept as literal?"

"I draw the line between the Old and New Testament. Anything in the New Testament, I would consider pretty much factual except for the obvious parables."

"But have you considered that there are 300 prophecies in the Old Testament that tell us about Christ, where and when He would come as the Messiah, etc.? If I'm not to believe these Old Testament miracles, then who's to say that the prophecies are true?"

He didn't have an answer.

"Do you believe the Red Sea story of how the waters parted for the Israelites to escape from the Egyptians?"

"Well," he said, "I just feel the water was shallow,

and they could have walked across on the high spots."

"That's strange," I answered, "because the Bible says that when Pharaoh's army of chariots and horsemen crossed, they were all drowned. Now how are you gonna' drown a horse, six or seven feet tall, in shallow water?"

He just looked at me dumb-like, his lips pressed tightly together.

Nick kept defending the Bible in class and when he'd get stumped he'd ask me questions, some of which I couldn't answer. So, I'd reach for the phone and call Pastor Lud. Of course, the class was a little bit awed by Nick's stand. He became known as the "Protestant." Some turned away from him, and I tried to encourage him, but Nick was learning at 13 what it meant to defend one's convictions.

He did well as a halfback in football that year. I always told him to put out even in practices--be the first one at the other end of the field when they ran sprints. The coaches were very rough, one even broke a finger on a kid's shoulder pad in the locker room at half-time. They were so intent on winning, they forgot principles. For instance, one day Nick told me that the freshmen team had won the game because they had played a sophomore who's name, ironically, was Virtue.

"The coach told us not to tell anybody or he'd kill us," Nick said.

"Nick, do you understand the implication here?" I asked him. "All your life you've played by the rules. Remember how we played by the rules in Little League? What, now that you're a freshman in high school we throw the rules away? You've got to make

The Making Of A Prophet

it right, and if you don't make it right, then I'm goin' to that school." I was really perturbed at the example those coaches were giving the kids.

He looked at me like he'd seen a ghost. "Okay, dad, I'll try," he said quickly.

Well, the day I knew he was going to speak to the coach, I called up Moody Bible's radio outreach and asked them to pray for a young Christian who was attempting to right a wrong.

When Nick came home that night he was smiling broadly. He had gone to the other team members that morning, told them what he had planned and asked their support. Not one offered to stand with him. In fact, they ridiculed him, calling him "holy Joe." So Nick, scared to death, went alone to see the coach before practice.

"Coach, I got to talk to you about playing sophomores in our games," he blurted out. Nick said the coach looked like he would explode.

"If you don't like the way I run this team then turn your gear in!" he yelled. Nick didn't know what to do and started praying as he went into the locker room. He got dressed for practice and went to the field. Again he went up to the coach, "Coach, I just want you to know that I can't play on this team if we're gonna' break the rules."

The coach looked at him a long time and then said, "Alright, if it makes you feel any better, we can work something else out."

So, Nick stayed on the team and scored some touchdowns that season, but for the rest of that year he was a marked man. In PE, when he'd goof off in exercises, a coach would come over and say, "Hey, I thought you were the guy that always followed the rules. You're not obeying rules right now. Forty push-ups."

At the final football banquet the head coach announced that because the freshmen team had played a sophomore, the school had to forfeit the game. Such experiences grew Nick up fast, and a little later on, when God sent me to evangelize the "street people," Nick, still a teen, stood at my side and ministered to people much older.

About this time I was in a barber shop and a manicurist who I had witnessed to several times grabbed me by the sleeve and said, "I want you to meet somebody." Waiting for a haircut was a nice looking guy who turned out to be a priest. The manicurist introduced us and I got right into telling him my story of conversion.

He interrupted me. "It sounds like you've been born again."

I said, "Father, you talk like a Baptist. How come you're talking this way?"

"I became born again myself about three years ago," he answered. "What happened was we had a guy like Billy Graham come to one of our retreats. He challenged all the priests to become true disciples and many of us had our lives changed that day."

"But how come you're still in a church that doesn't teach this experience?"

He said, "Well, someone's going to have to reach all those Catholics on Sunday morning." God taught me through that experience that He has those who really love Him in every denomination.

As I continued to try to deal with people about faith,

The Making Of A Prophet

God began to deal with me. Rather than argue about which denomination was the right one, I felt He wanted me to bring them closer to Him by sharing my experiences. If their light wasn't shining as bright as mine, they would know it and would move toward or away from it. Through the years I've met many "born again" Catholics. They perhaps didn't use that expression but their commitment to Christ was obvious from their lives.

Do I believe some denominations have more truth than others? Absolutely. Usually the church or organization that really believes the Bible is God's message to His chosen people, will have less erroneous doctrine.

One day the Lord spoke to me about those printing companies I had cheated in order to get to Hollywood. With great apprehension I began calling on them, and typically, a sales manager would say, "Ah, don't worry about it. Just send $100 to the United Jewish Relief, or the American Cancer Society." Every time God asked me to return stolen property, ask forgiveness, or make restitution to someone, it always worked out.

One day I met Dave Thiesen who was very active with the Chicago Christian Businessmen. I would get up begrudgingly at 5:00 in the morning to go to a prayer breakfast with him to give my testimony. I was an oddity to protestant businessmen because I had been "saved" in a Catholic church.

One morning, Dave, in his typical challenging way, said, "You ought to go with us to Cook County jail some Sunday." The first time I went I had to go to the bathroom about five times, I was so nervous. But I was to find, as I have so often since, that all God was asking me to do was take that *first step* of faith and He would go with me and give me the words to say, just like He promised in His Word.

The old Cook County jail is formidable looking. At least a hundred years old, it reminds you of an old fort. You enter it through large double doors that open to an outer hallway where visitors wait to visit the inmates inside. This is where all the Sunday teams meet, have prayer, and worship before ministering. This is where the Lord seemed to meet us in a special way I had yet to experience sitting in a church. It's not hard to understand when you remember the Lord's words, "I was in prison, and you came to me."

Mother York, a tiny black pastor evangelist and jail chaplain, usually led the service. No matter how jittery you felt going in, her peppery encouragement and love hugs somehow took the "self" out of you and you were ready to do battle.

On that first visit, our team of four businessmen went into a cell block and found about 40 young Blacks sitting around watching TV, playing cards, or doing pushups. We opened with a song, and I kept a watchful eye out for a possible bucket of water coming our way.

The men asked me to speak. I nervously told how Christ had given me a new lease on life. Another man gave an invitation to accept Christ and about 20 Blacks went down on their knees. After that you couldn't keep me out of that jail. I served in that ministry for the next 20 years.

But not every Sunday was so successful. Sometimes we were shouted down by Black Muslims who wanted Allah to have more than equal time with Jesus. Sometimes, the TV would be turned up to drown us out. The guards tried to keep order, but they were spread pretty

The Making Of A Prophet

thin. To their credit, the wardens through the years welcomed the Sunday teams as a positive influence and helped them in various ways.

As our three oldest children turned 18, they all went to Cook with me occasionally--Nick going the most often. Paul Schoenthal, who married Rita, became a team captain and served faithfully for several years. When we heard that Tommy Hicks, linebacker for the Chicago Bears, had accepted Christ, we had him as a guest and the prisoners were deeply touched by his testimony.

When I heard that Dick Gregory, comedian turned activist whom I had met previously, had been locked up on a civil disobedience charge and was on a hunger strike, I went to his cell block to encourage and pray with him. He remembered me and seemed very touched that I had sought him out. I don't remember his "cause" at the time, but I had to take my hat off to anyone who could turn his back on a successful career in show business and devote his time to helping society.

One Sunday, Marie Elkins, a tall majestic Negro lady with graying hair and a head held high and eyes that have seen too much hardship to be able to express so much love, came as a guest. The first cell block we visited, a dozen or so Blacks were lounging around. Marie began: "Mornin' children," she shouted over the blaring TV. "We come this mornin' to sing with you and tell you about the Lord Jesus. Won't someone come over and shake my hand? I loves you. Jesus loves you. Won't you come?"

No response, except for the four playing poker in a far corner who tossed some wise cracks our way. The

TV continued its opposition and no one moved to switch it off.

Next, we sang a few songs, mostly to ourselves. I read scripture and someone else related how Christ had changed his life, but it was Marie who was chosen by God for this hour. We wondered how she could ever get their attention. She took a deep breath, and with eyes closed and face to the ceiling, she began to pray. One by one the prisoners turned our way, aware they were hearing real, gut-level, eye-filling, heart rendering prayer--not rambling words, not a disguised sermon.

When I opened my eyes, a young Black was walking toward us. He walked right up to the bars and sat down on the single stool directly in front of us, all the time staring at Marie. It was the most beautiful example of the Holy Spirit's drawing power imaginable.

Marie offered him her hand. He hesitated, then accepted.

"Hello, son," she said, softly.

He mumbled something.

"You know Jesus loves you, don't you?"

He nodded.

"Would you like to give Him your life today?"

The boy's expression was beginning to soften. "It's hard," he whispered.

"Sure, it's hard. Acceptin' Jesus is always hard. We don't know what to expect. We're so used to bein' in control of ourselves we expect the worse if we even let go for a minute. But we can never know Him till we're willin' to turn over our control center to Him.

Tears were beginning down the boy's cheeks. The other prisoners had turned the TV down and were starting to listen. Marie prayed with him. After some

The Making Of A Prophet

long quiet minutes, a radiance began to fill his face. He eagerly accepted the Bible we handed him. The atmosphere in the room continued to be subdued.

I noticed a big guy with a scarred up face with no shirt on and quite muscular sitting alone and taking everything in with a forlorn expression. I had turned away to get some Bibles to hand out and when I straightened up, the man was standing a foot away, his forehead pressed against the bars. His body odor and breath could knock you over.

"Can God forgive someone who commits murder?" he asked me, quietly. Marie, just finishing with the young lad, turned and said, "Son, don't you know Moses committed murder? God forgave him and used him in a mighty way."

"Yes, but I killed my sister-in-law," he said.

"Child, God sees no difference in sin," Marie said. "The Bible says all have sinned and have come short of the glory of God. The only difference between you and me right now is that I have asked for the precious blood of Jesus to cover my sins and you have not. Am I speakin' the truth?"

"Yes," he said, looking at the floor.

"Would you like to ask Jesus to cover these sins right now?"

"Yes," he answered, just above a whisper.

Again Marie prayed and now others were approaching the bars to make it right with their Creator.

After I grew used to the various ways Satan tried to oppose us in jail I really enjoyed preaching because though I didn't fully realize it, I was using the gift God had given me to further His Kingdom. One morning I was preaching my heart out and a Mexican, Paul

McCoy, who had been busted countless times for using narcotics, accepted Christ. Brother Speck and others had a hand in his turn-about also.

He finally got out on parole and one night a friend crashed at his place and overdosed on heroin during the night. When Paul awoke the police were searching him and they found narcotics in the room. In Illinois that constitutes possession.

I believed he was innocent and wanted to testify at his trial about his changed character but I wasn't allowed to. An officer let me speak with him while the jury was out. I asked Paul, "What are you going to do if they find you guilty?"

He smiled that big wide smile and said, "Ron, whatever God wants is okay with me. I'm in His hands." Paul McCoy was a free man no matter what the world did to him.

The jury brought in a guilty verdict and he was sent to Joliet prison. Every time I'd visit him there, he'd tell me about someone else he had led to the Lord. He was reaching men who you couldn't drag to church on Sunday.

I began to do consistent witnessing wherever I went. If the Bible were true then I was compelled to tell everyone who would listen that there was a heaven and hell. Recently, I heard a taped testimony by Howard Pittman when he was preaching in Springdale, Arkansas. On August 3, 1979, he suffered a massive heart attack and was pronounced dead on the way to the hospital. While doctors tried to revive him, he had an out-of-body experience. He was caught up into heaven and had an encounter with Jesus Christ. He was told that even though he was a born again preacher, much

The Making Of A Prophet

of his work had been *for* Christ but not *with* Christ. He was told that he would be given another chance to work *with* Christ on earth if he would be truly obedient to the Holy Spirit. Many things were revealed to him, but the most important to me was the revelation that in an actual 15 minutes of earth's time, 50 souls from all around the world died and were ushered to heaven with much rejoicing. But, during that same time period, almost 2,000 other souls died and were ushered into hell. I thought about that taped message for days.

I began to witness more frequently. The devil would speak to me again and again that I was jeopardizing my income as a salesman. But one day I was having lunch with a sales promotion manager, the first time I ever met him. I was prompted to speak to him about Christ and what He had done for me. Halfway through the meal he stopped and said, "You know Ron, I've got to tell you something. This is incredible. I almost committed suicide a year ago and since then I've been meeting with a Lutheran minister. Your story is a great encouragement. If God can do all that for you then He can certainly do something for me."

When I arrived home that evening I was still on cloud nine and at supper I told the family about my wonderful experience. But what happened to me next was so profound, so mind blowing, that never again would I be able to look at my fellow man in the same way.

THREE

"LUD, WHAT'S HAPPENING TO ME?" I asked Pastor Lud Golz, the fundamentalist pastor that had taken me under his wing. He and I had been praying in his office on a Saturday morning for others we were concerned about when a heaviness came over me, and I began to sob.

"God's touching you," he answered.

But after ten minutes elapsed and the heaviness had not passed, I cried, "I can't handle it." Lud began to pray for me. The heaviness began to subside and the Lord gave me this message: *No one is doing enough to reach the unsaved.* That meant Lud, me, the church, everyone. Lud asked me to speak on Sunday to the congregation and sadly, the message seemed to have little effect, although I believe Lud was deeply touched. But I'll tell you this, my life changed. Overnight I became strongly motivated to reach the lost, especially the youth. I know now that I received the baptism in the Holy Spirit that morning and it was for power to be more effective in witnessing. No matter what you call it: second blessing, charismatic renewal, or being spirit filled, it's real, though many Christians don't believe it's for them--especially fundamentalists. What they don't like to hear is that Torrey, D.L. Moody, and Finney all believed and taught that the baptism in the Holy Spirit was for modern day Christians just as in Jesus' time. But *I've* received it and make no apology because it is scriptural. Jesus told the apostles to wait in Jerusalem for the power that would come from on high and that they were to preach to all nations, beginning at Jerusalem. (Luke 24:47-49) And that's exactly what happened in the second chapter of Acts.

I did not speak in tongues that morning for whatever reason, but a year later the Lord sent Wil Ogden and Cas Knoester to counsel and lay hands on me, and praise the Lord, it happened! I know now that it is possible to be baptized in the Holy Spirit and not speak in another language. Cas made it so plain; just as when I stepped out in faith for salvation and for healing, this had to come by faith too. By faith, I had to open my mouth and speak--it was the Holy Spirit who gave the utterance.

Much bolder now, I visited nearby towns at night and passed out gospel tracts by the thousands. Those most receptive were the youth. This was during the troubled sixties and many kids were disillusioned with dope, booze, sex, or just materialism and were desperate to get some meaning into their lives. Arthur Blessitt and Duane Pederson in California and other concerned Christians had been street preaching across the country and in 1967 the Holy Spirit began to fall on young people, most of whom were unchurched.

On a Saturday afternoon 60 to 70 Catholics meeting at Notre Dame, hardly knowing who the Holy Spirit was, began to weep and praise God in a new way as the Spirit was poured out. Their meetings exploded in

The Making Of A Prophet

number overnight and today, there are hundreds of thousands of Catholic Charismatics in the US.

I found that my boldness and conviction got a kid's attention. Before long a small group of young guys were going out with me and somehow the name "Jesus freaks" was put on us. The early freaks, the beatniks, reacted to a conforming middle-class society that told kids, "Don't make waves, get an education, a master's degree, a wife with the same cultural background and nationality, work for a corporation, retire at 62, and die happy." The freaks saw our ills, but not the cures. "Get love," the early ones yelled with flowers in their hair--till everyone saw we needed something more than man's self attempts at love. "Get peace," the next wave yelled, and admittedly, napalm bombs were a devastating indictment on Americans. But while 70,000 Americans died in Viet Nam, 143,000 died from drug abuse at home. (*US News and World Report,* August, 1970.)

"Get lost," another group yelled. "Get out of a sick society and live in a commune in the mountains." But long hair, living common law, and eating organically-grown carrots did not satisfy that vague emptiness deep inside, as many who have been on that trip have testified. "Get dope," became another desperate cry, but here too, bum trips, friends who overdosed, wiped-out minds, or living with paranoia of getting busted, just made the whole thing a bummer.

At first the youth thought we were another religious cult like the Krishnas, Ba'hai, or Buddha, or even worse, middle-class, white-color churchianity. When they found Jesus loved them just the way they were and wouldn't force them into a socially acceptable lifestyle, they really turned on. Some of them came out of a hellish world where a revelation of Satan while "tripping" often happened.

In Jesus, they found the freedom they had been searching so hard for--the power He had promised that would enable them to beat enslaving habits, stop messing up people they cared for; get rid of that sin monkey on their backs, or do what they knew they should do, but couldn't because they were powerless.

Like one beggar telling another beggar where to find bread, they spread the word that Jesus had come to town with a basket large enough to feed every street person who wanted freedom more than anything. The movement spread like fire--holy fire! Up and down Sunset Strip in LA, in Atlanta, Chicago suburbs, Milwaukee, and other towns. Jesus people yelled "get saved" and "Jesus loves you" to a world aimlessly wandering by just working to eat and waiting to die.

Some of them put on sackcloth and ashes and pounded staffs against the sidewalk in protest outside strip bars and Go-Go joints. There was no sacred ground. People were presented with the gospel coming out of churches, at shopping malls, even at the 1971 Billy Graham Crusade at McCormick Place in Chicago. The Lord told us to take our nine-foot wooden cross to that crusade and put "Jesus Loves You" stickers on Bible-toting Christians--many of whom refused them. Later that same evening Satan worshippers attempted to disrupt the meeting at the invitation only to find the Jesus people blocking their way. Graham's right-hand man later came out to thank us personally.

Not all the Jesus people were ex-freaks. Many came from lukewarm churches, where they wanted deeper things of God than they were getting. Mainline church

The Making Of A Prophet

goers were uncomfortable with their fanaticism, but they had a zeal for Jesus that said, "Before you come down heavy on my unorthodox ways, at least be as sold out as I am." There wasn't anything new about the Jesus freak when you looked at history. St. Francis, Luther, Finney, and Jesus, Himself, were considered radicals. In a fanatical society where people scream their lungs out at a ballgame or beat each other up over a hockey game, it sometimes takes a fanatic to get attention. For too long Christians have fought a defensive warfare. For too long have they said the name "Jesus" apologetically. While mainline denominations slept, the Jesus freak went out and evangelized.

Possessions were a hassle he didn't want. With a coat, a sleeping bag, and a Bible, he was ready to move anywhere, anytime, just like the apostles. He got heard and he said a lot to a desperate sin-sick society through every channel available--even the news media, which never dreamed its magazines and talk shows were being used by God to witness to the multitudes.

The local church seemed the logical place to stir those newly converted, but *not* into a youth fellowship where pee-wee golf, go-karting, or tobogganing with a prayer thrown in once in awhile was the practice. Recently, I read about a practice in an Indiana church called "toothbrush buffet" where each youth group member brushes his teeth and spits into a cup, then passes it on for the next to do the same. The last one drinks down everyone's spit. What do teens learn from such stupid games? Of course, nothing of the Bible, or theology, or the cost of discipleship. But they do learn other things that will stay with them through life such as: losing inhibitions--most teens have problems doing anything too embarrassing, or giving into peer pressure and going along with the group, no matter the cost--just the opposite of Christ's teaching about standing up to the whole world, alone if need be, to defend one's faith.

So, out of frustration, we started our own meetings in our home and in a short time were averaging 100 kids on a Sunday night. They came from the streets, from the local churches, some, from many miles away. We called ourselves "Jesus is Lord" fellowship, and we taught the fundamentals over and over: commitment to Christ, water baptism, baptism in the Holy Spirit, and discipleship. Some who came were demon-possessed which was uncovered as they drew closer to the cross. I knew then why God had baptized me with His Spirit a couple of years earlier. No way could I have continued the ministry without it, because this was no "taffy-pull" but head-on *warfare* with Satan.

I remember one night we baptized a young gal who, when she came out of the water sank to the ground and kept saying, "Get away from me!" Her left arm moved out from her body as if she were being pulled as she continued yelling to be left alone. Those present came against Satan in the name of Jesus Christ. When she recovered she told us that when she came out of the water tremendous oppression hit her. She felt Satan wanted her body--he wanted her physically. But she said as we prayed for her, she felt a real release and knew now that she was free. We admonished her to keep her house cleansed and swept so that demons might not enter again.

Many Christians believe a Christian cannot be demon-possessed but it's very obvious as you talk to

The Making Of A Prophet

these objectors how little actual experience they've had. They cannot prove by the Bible that a Christian cannot be demon-possessed. "Be Spirit filled," Paul says, and that means one hundred percent. Most Christians are not.

In our experience we found that many of the young people who have dealt in the occult will reveal some form of satanic oppression. In case you didn't realize it, a large percentage of schools in America are offering courses on occultism under titles like *"Studies on the Supernatural."* Transcendental Meditation, which is really an eastern cult teaching, is offered in schools as *"Science of Creative Intelligence"* (SCI). If it's taboo to teach students the gospel of Christ, then these other religions should be outlawed too.

Our experience has shown that demon oppression, and even possession, can occur if a person insists on holding envy, jealousy, pride, resentment, hatred, rebellion, or addictions, which often lead to depression, sickness, self destruction, and even suicide.

It must be said too, that there is a danger in attributing all human problems to demons. You can cast out a demon but you cannot cast out man's carnal nature. But make no mistake, demon-possession is real! Because many people are fearful of things beyond their understanding, they choose to ignore the evidence and go on living tormented lives; yet, much of the ministry of Christ was devoted to casting devils out of people.

One day, Ken Downey, thirty years old and itching for a ministry after several years of comparative inactivity in a local fundamentalist church, came to a meeting and decided working with kids was where God wanted him. But first God had to de-program him and his loving wife, Carolyn, from the teaching they had sat under since conversion. Their doubts about the validity of the baptism in the Holy Spirit vanished the night they received it. Their doubts about instantaneous physical healing and miracles vanished the first time they saw someone healed miraculously on the spot. After awhile the ministry became very demanding. Because of their wisdom and knowledge of scripture Ken and Carolyn became excellent counselors.

Several in our group attended Bill Gothard's Basic Youth Conflicts Seminar about this time and though I believe this gifted teacher gave us timely insights into youth and family problems, I felt his stand against music with a beat, and even Christian rock, was heavy handed, and his lack of teaching on miraculous signs and wonders didn't help the thousands of fundamentalists who were sadly lacking in this gospel truth and swooned at his feet. But, of course, he was raised in dispensationalism that teaches miracles that happened in New Testament times do not occur today.

Signs and wonders began for us as a result of an "airlift" to Scandinavia with the Full Gospel Businessmen, where I witnessed many miracles. Absolutely the most outstanding was the Pelletier miracle. If my memory serves me, this happened in Copenhagen, Denmark, about 1968 or '69. A man named Pelletier introduced his very young son to the audience at our evening service and then asked if anyone had something his boy could read. My son, Nick, and I were sitting with other ministers on stage directly behind the man. Nick jumped up, gave Mr. Pelletier his passport, and the boy read Nick's statistics out loud.

What was so unusual, was that the boy was reading

The Making Of A Prophet

from a sightless eye. Earlier, the man had bandaged the good eye and asked those on stage to inspect the wrapping. Also interesting, is that before reading the passport the boy removed a plastic eyeball from his eye socket. Never will I forget the reaction from the audience. People screamed and stomped their feet and called out loudly to Jesus, praising Him again and again.

Because this is such a remarkable miracle, I thought you'd like to know some of the details of its history. The following is in Mr. Pelletier's own words:

> In July of 1968, my oldest of four sons, who was then five, suffered a severe, freakish injury to his left eye. David Jr. was hospitalized over a month with eye specialists trying to save the eye. Although thousands were praying for God to perform a miracle, it was not God's will, and the complete eyeball with the optic nerve was removed in August of 1968.
>
> A few days following this, God spoke to my heart with complete assurance that the reason he did not perform the miracle for which people were praying was that He had a greater miracle to perform--giving David sight even without a physical eye. I knew with full faith that someday this revelation would become a reality.
>
> The miracle occurred July 6, 1971, three years later, at 10 p.m. Davey had been in bed but not yet asleep. He ran down the hall, bounded into the living room where guests were visiting with us, and shouted, "Mama, Daddy, I can see out of my bad eye," which is what he called it. I knew at the moment of David's proclamation that my faith had been answered, and God's revelation of three years before had come to pass. I would not have even had to test him, but for the fact of the guests in our home who were utterly agape

at the circumstances.

Upon examination, with the good eye completely covered, David was able to see the light from three lamps on in the room, and he pointed to them, and even touched their shades. He also identified my comb held in front of one of the lamps. We praised God for His wonderful miracle to us!

Since that first night, David's vision has improved to where he not only has light perception, but can see objects, forms, colors, movement; *and he can even read*. Of course it makes absolutely no difference whether the plastic eye is in or out. He sees with a "spiritual eye" through the mighty power of a loving Lord who is every bit as able and desirous of performing miracles now as He did when he walked the shores of Galilee.

Several eye surgeons have verified and certified this miracle. Other eye specialists have shown complete bewilderment and expressed the opinion it might be ESP. A simple experiment disproves ESP. David is unable to see the object chosen if it is held too far left or right of his left eye. David is seeing through a sort of tunnel or flashlight-ray vision. With ESP, it would make no difference where the object were placed.

God gave us this miracle when we needed it the most, and we give our Lord all the glory. It is nothing we have done. I can't even take credit for the faith.

People are receiving Jesus Christ into their lives through this miracle. Lives are being changed. Christians are being revived and quickened. People who have seldom thought about God are seriously considering Him. Hardened men whose hearts are cold are breaking under the love and power of God they see in this miracle--the same power to forgive a man's sins and save his soul. God has given me ministries by mail, over the phone, and in personal contact, the most

The Making Of A Prophet

effective ministry I've ever had. People just are not the same after seeing the miracle! Many are waking up to the fact that the Christ of the New Testament is the same today, willing and able to do the same miracles and healings as we unwaveringly trust Him for them. Today they can be harvesting equipment to bring men and women to Christ, who simply cannot be reached in any other way but to see a demonstration of the spectacular power of god.

In my opinion, this is the only type of miracle that when demonstrated to various groups in various geographical areas is on-the-spot proof of a miracle and God's power at work. Healings of the lame, the deaf, those with cancer, etc., simply could not have the effective testimony except among one's acquaintances. Many would not believe, because there would be no *visible* proof. But when you see a young lad seeing out of an empty socket while the good eye is completely covered--what an irrefutable testimony of God's love and peace.

I personally feel time is short; these are the last days; Christ's return for His redeemed is near. And in these last days, He has promised a mighty outpouring of His Holy Spirit. I feel the miracle of David's vision is the beginning of great things to come in these last days, that there are many miracles to come. God may choose you to work them through, as you yield your life to Christ and completely trust Him.

> In Christ,
> Dave and Doris Pelletier

P.S. When Davey was asked by newsmen what the miracle meant to him, his answer was so simple and beautiful--"That Jesus loves me."

God has given us discernment to demonstrate the miracle only to those He wants to see it. We recall that

> Christ did not do many miracles in Nazareth because of their unbelief. (Matthew 13:58)
>
> We are being very careful not to exploit David, but at the same time we want the most people to know, in the best way, the miracle was for the glory of God.
>
> The day after the miracle, a minister from Ohio and his wife and three children whom we hadn't seen in years visited us, and completely unaware of the miracle, told us that two of his children had been praying for three years, without missing a night, that David would be able to see again out of the eyeless socket. Through tears of joy, we told them that the miracle happened last night and gave a demonstration. God's power came down. The children's faith was rewarded.

On the flight home from Scandinavia I taped an interview with Drummon Thom, an evangelist with signs and wonders, and played the tape at our next Sunday night meeting. At the tape's conclusion a young student from Judson College told me she suffered from a bad back and had a short leg. She asked me to pray for her sometime. I told her I would, but at break time the Lord said to me, *pray now for her, not later.*

I was sure I wasn't hearing right and tried to ignore the thought. But it wouldn't go away. (You've been there, huh?) Finally, willing to do anything to get some peace, I went to my bedroom, shut the door, and dropped to my knees. "Lord, are you sure?" I cried out to him. "What if nothing happens when I pray? What will those kids think?" And I knew immediately that losing their respect was what I was really afraid of. The Lord seemed to say *just trust me,* and I realized it was another *first step* of faith I was being asked to take. With a new surge of faith, I went back to the group and said, "Okay, people, listen up. God's about

The Making Of A Prophet

to do a miracle."

I sat the Judson girl in a straight-back chair and asked her to extend her legs. I held her heels in my palm, and sure enough, one leg was about three-quarters of an inch shorter. I said a short prayer, and of course, nothing happened. *Now I've done it,* I thought to myself. About to panic, I decided to try one more time. "Lord," I cried loudly, "I saw You do it in Sweden, I know You can do it!" Just then, the leg slowly grew out before our eyes. The place went up for grabs!

I smile now as I reflect on why it didn't move the instant I prayed. Was the Lord waiting for faith to rise to a certain level in the room? Was there a spiritual war going on between spirits of skepticism, doubt and faith? Or, was the Lord demonstrating that He has a sense of humor? Someday, perhaps sooner than I know, I will find out.

Four others had limbs lengthened that night, helping their lower back pains. Other ailments were cured also. You could have preached 10,000 words and not gotten the faith those miracles produced that night.

As older people began attending our meetings, we began to pray for the sick regularly and God healed many. But it was the young people who seemed more willing to take God at His Word that were touched most often. One night I received a call from Jim Carter, a student at Judson College, who was in great pain.

"The nurse says I've got appendicitis and that I've got to go to the hospital right away. But in James, it says to call the elders and you're my elder, so what should I do?"

"Seek the Lord till we get there. We're leaving right now."

Ken was busy, so grabbing the anointing oil I drove to Judson, about twenty minutes away. The Lord began to remind me of verses of scripture that would help Jim's faith for healing.

The kids from Judson who attended our meetings met me in Jim's room. They had been praying and were anticipating great things, and I knew the responsibility I bore since his condition seemed critical. He was lying on his bed and I knelt down beside him.

"You really want to believe the Lord, huh?"

"Yeah," he smiled, through pain.

"You know, Jim, God can heal you without me or Ken, don't you? I mean, if we hadn't been available, what would you have done?"

"I guess the Holy Spirit would have told me something else to do; all I know is He told me to call you."

"Okay. Obedience is what God is after. But my point is, someday the elders won't be around. It's not *our* faith that should carry you, do you understand?"

"Yes."

"Okay, I'm going to give you two verses that I want you to think about. In Deuteronomy 28:61, God said to Israel, '...every sickness, and every plague, which is not written in the book of this Law, them will the Lord bring upon thee, until thou be destroyed.' God was warning the Israelites to give up their wickedness or be cursed, and we see that people get sick today because they're still under that curse. Notice He said, 'sickness not written in this book,' and that means appendicitis. Now look at Galatians 3:13. 'Christ has redeemed us from the curse of the Law, being made a curse for us:

The Making Of A Prophet

for it is written, cursed is everyone that hangs on a tree.' Follow so far?"

"Sure."

"Now here's what I want you to do. Say this little sentence over and over to yourself. According to Deuteronomy 28:61, appendicitis is a curse of the Law, but according to Galatians 3:13, Christ redeemed me from that curse of the Law, therefore, I am free from the curse and refuse to carry this appendicitis any longer."

After I anointed him with oil we let him alone. When he came into the room fifteen minutes later he was all smiles. The pain was gone completely! And it never returned!

But was everyone healed that we prayed for? No. Do I believe that when people are not healed, it is always because of lack of faith or unconfessed sin? No. Many times preachers are guilty of playing the devil's advocate by telling people to jump off the temple as the devil tried to get Jesus to do. "I've prayed for you, now take off your glasses." It doesn't make any difference if your driver's license says you must wear them and you still can't see. Or, since you have been prayed for, you are healed of diabetes and don't have to take insulin even though the symptoms are still there. But the symptoms sometimes turn into harsh reality. We must come to understand the whole counsel of God. Jesus knew that if He cast himself off the temple He would be committing the sin of presumption in tempting the Lord God. Not even He had the right to do that. The other side of the sin of presumption is the sin of unbelief. In between lies the golden thread of faith.

Ron Rendleman

There are two Greek words which show the difference between faith and presumption: one is *rayma*, the other *logos*. Both mean "Word" in the New Testament. Rayma is God's Word to you, personally. Logos is God's Word to all men. How many times have you read a Bible verse and it didn't mean a lot to you--that's *logos*. But one day God speaks a word to you that sinks into your spirit--the *logos* becomes *rayma* and if you need healing you will be healed.

So, how should we approach healing? First, denounce dispensational teaching if you have sat under it. Tell God of your unbelief if you suffer from that, and ask Him to give you a measure of faith and confess to others what you are believing God for. When symptoms get severe don't feel guilty about seeing a doctor (after really seeking God of course). If you are never healed, don't get bitter and say to God, "God, if I had a son who was doing all he could to serve You, I wouldn't treat him like You've treated me." Just remember, friend, how God *did* treat His Son, Jesus Christ. What God does to us may not always seem fair.

Anyway, back to the story. I received the inspiration to produce rock concerts that would be evangelistic and lift up Christ. Again, I was being asked to take another *first step* of faith. I didn't have much money or the foggiest notion how to start, and the local churches didn't seem interested. But I knew that a gospel quartet singing songs written in the 19th century would never appeal to the kids I wanted to reach. So, I contacted Jesus rock groups like "Hope," "Sheep," "Morning Glory," "Homeward Bound," and my favorite--the "E" band. Greg Volz and the crew of the "E" band worked all week at factory jobs and often traveled 200 miles on weekends to play their original music and many times received barely enough to cover expenses. I have seldom met more devoted Christians anywhere.

The first concert was at the College of DuPage in Wheaton, Illinois. They told me I couldn't preach, but "Crimson Bridge" did a great job presenting a positive witness, and many of the kids from the college and surrounding schools went away touched, I'm sure.

We tried to hold concerts outdoors if at all possible, and only God knows how many thousands are in the Kingdom today because of a Jesus rock concert. We probably had more conversions of youth during that period than all the Chicago suburban churches put together. I don't say this to brag but to show that God doesn't need elaborate programs or huge amounts of money to reach the lost--one man will do just fine--one man (or woman) willing to take that *first step* of faith.

Jerry Harvey from Aurora called me one day. He had just gotten out of seminary. He said, "Ron, I understand you put on concerts. I'd like to put one on for the kids in Aurora. We've got a real need here. There's a lot of dope on the streets and I just feel a concert would be timely." We prayed together and received the go-ahead.

So Jerry and a handful of kids from the "Mustard Seed," a Jesus house he headed up, began distributing handbills. The Lord said, "If I be lifted up, I'll draw all men to myself." Consequently, we were never ashamed of Jesus in our advertising.

That night in Aurora was memorable! I stood before 1500 kids and said, "Listen, man, remember one thing: If you want to follow Jesus, it's going to take some guts. You're going to have to make a stand. If you want to come up here right now and say, 'Jesus, I'll follow you,' then I'll know your Christianity is going to start off on the right foot, and you'll have the courage to tell someone else about Christ tomorrow. It's not the Peace corps we're trying to sell you, it isn't a better life, it could be the hardest life you'll ever try to live. But it will be the most fulfilling, and you can be sure that you're going to heaven when your time comes."

In my preaching, I tried not to appeal just to people's emotions but to make sure they had counted the cost. We used music as a gate to enter their souls, but preaching showed them their sins and that they needed a Savior. Some evangelists only work on the mind and produce intellectual "fruit," and some work hard on emotion, but we tried to hit the conscience heavily and consequently, the will. We had gotten free from the numbers game.

Among those who came up, eyes tearing, that night was a 14-year-old boy named Mario. We told the kids we'd have a baptism in the Fox River the next day--we always tried to baptize soon as possible after conversion. We even began to haul around an old horse trough, painted bright red, in our van.

Well we had the baptism but Mario didn't show up. He drowned while swimming that same day. Jerry told me that when they laid Mario in the casket, they put the little Bible and follow-up material we passed out at the concert in his hands. Mario made it all right, but he came within 24 hours of *not* making it.

TOP: Elder Ken Downey baptizing a new convert.
BOTTOM: The Jesus People ministering at a Billy Graham crusade at Chicago's McCormick Place.

TOP: Our "Homeward Bound" singers. Left to right: Paul Oyen, Becky Dohogne, Rita Rendleman, Gil Evans.
BOTTOM: The Jesus People "Harvest" band tries to keep up with a rockin' Salvation Army group in Stockholm.

TOP: Taking the Gospel to Chicago's Civic Center.
BOTTOM: The "E" band. Left to right: Joe Grier, Dave Eden, Tom Byler, Dave O'Haner, Greg Volz.

Ron preaching to street people at a Jesus Rock Concert in Lombard, Illinois.

FOUR

SOME GIRLS AT WHEATON COLLEGE who attended our meetings began praying that I'd be able to speak in their chapel. I thought they were crazy. It would take a miracle. I was fast getting a reputation of being radical, but these girls, Doneetsa, Nancy, and others wouldn't give up. And not much later, I received an invitation from the chaplain to speak. On a day hard to forget, about 400 people were present. Part of what I said follows:

"It's my conviction that there are many Christian practices today that are not in God's Plan A, but Plan B. What do I mean? Highest will, permissive will. Look at Exodus 4:14. Moses is arguing with God. You know the story. Moses did not want to lead his people. He kept saying, 'I can't do it. I can't do it. I stutter. I this, I that.' So God said, 'Aaron will become your spokesman.' Plan B went into effect.

"1st Samuel 8:7 illustrates another turning point in the history of the Israelites. It was not God's highest will that they should have kings. And the Lord said unto Samuel, 'They have not rejected thee, but they have rejected Me. Hearken unto their voice and make them a king, that I should not reign over them. Plan B.

"Remember what Jesus said in Mark 10? 'From the beginning it was not so. For the hardness of your heart, Moses wrote a bill of divorcement and from the beginning of creation God made them male and female.' Plan A was that there was not to be a divorce.

"So, I put forth a proposition. Many of us think because we're born in a Christian home, go to an evangelical church, and on to a Christian college, we are automatically in Plan A of God. I'm not saying you can't be in Plan A, but what I'm wondering about is how many of you just supposed you were, but aren't? Let me give you some areas where I really feel Christians are not in God's Plan A.

"Number One: Healing. In James, 'If there are any sick among you call the elders of the church, let them pray over him, anointing him with oil in the name of the Lord and the prayer of faith *shall save the sick*.' It doesn't say call the AMA, it doesn't say run for a flu shot or go get aspirins, it says call the elders and they will anoint you.

"Number Two: Church services that feature one man Sunday after Sunday. I Corinthians 14:25, 'How is it then brethren, when you come together *every one of you* has a psalm, a tongue, a revelation, an interpretation.' Plan A is the New Testament church. Plan B is what a church service has evolved into today.

"Number Three: The gospel, and the way it's preached today. What is the true great commission? I ask you to look at Matthew 10:7 and 8 with a prayerful heart, and tell me if this doesn't say something to you. Jesus is speaking: 'As you go, preach that the kingdom of heaven is at hand. Heal the sick, cleanse the lepers, raise the dead, cast out devils, freely you have received, freely give.' And what are we preaching today? Half a gospel. The whole gospel is that Christ not only saves, but He delivers, heals, baptizes with the Holy Spirit, and causes us to be overcomers, *if we believe.*

"A year ago a brother came to our meeting and said, 'Hey, aren't you baptizing your converts?' I'd never thought of it. He said, 'Don't you know your scriptures?' And he began to take us step-by-step through the Book of Acts. Do you know that in nine places in the Book of Acts where they reached somebody, they baptized him immediately? They didn't wait until the pastor was ready. They didn't wait until April, according to their church tradition. They did it immediately.

"Number Four: Christian families without a spiritual head--the father, who has been replaced by the pastor, Sunday school, or colleges. Did you ever stop to think that the spiritual truth that you're getting in this school should have been taught to you by your father? Plan B.

"Number Five: Women missionaries are Plan B. What? God made woman to be a helpmate. He didn't make her a jungle fighter. Listen, Kathryn Kuhlman stood on the stage before a crowd of 5,000 people, turned to the pastors and businessmen sitting up on the stage and said, 'I know I'm not God's highest will for this work. One of you men missed the calling of the Holy Spirit in your life.' I'm not suggesting every woman missionary or worker lay down her tools and go home. God has called and blessed many women to the field, but I believe He does so because of the lack of dedicated men. We noticed this particularly at Cook County jail where mighty black women of God were raised up when black ministers ignored that ministry.

"Number Six: Education. I think education for education's sake is Plan B. As a Christian, everything you do should be centered around Christ. Every activity, every course that you take should help you be a better disciple. Ask yourself: 'Since I've come to college, am I closer to Christ than before?'

"Paul wrote in I Corinthians 3:19: 'For the wisdom of this world is foolishness before God.' And later he wrote, 'Where is the wise man, the philosopher? Where is the scribe, the scholar, where is the investigator, the logician, the debater of this present time and age? Has not God shown up the nonsense and the folly of this world's wisdom? By the way, what did Paul do when he needed to make a buck? He made tents. He didn't fall back on his education at all. He used his hands.

"'Hey, God, I built a computer that helped send Americans into space.'

"And God answered, 'But how did you further My kingdom? Did you really think you furthered My kingdom by helping Americans explore space?'

"Does a man commit mental suicide when he becomes a disciple of Christ? No. Your first obligation for studying is found in Joshua. 'This book of the Law shall not depart out of thy mouth but thou shall meditate therein day and night that thou mayest observe to do according to all that is written therein; for then thou shalt make thy way prosperous, and then thou shalt have good success.'

"In other words, God's ways must be your ways. But if you're so programmed from morning to night with school activities that you can't think straight, how can you study God's Word? Education has become a sacred cow to many of you. You are worshipping the almighty "A". That's idol worship, and God says that's an abomination.

"The reasons why I cannot counsel young people to attend college today and why my own children did not go are: First of all, loans are wrong. Some of you people are deeply in debt and will be for a long time. Proverbs 22:7: 'The rich rule over the poor; the borrower is servant to the lender.' God doesn't want you to be a servant to anybody except Jesus Christ.

"Secondly, many courses are irrelevant while many professors are atheists in secular schools or nominal Christians in Christian schools. They're not going to teach my kids.

"Third reason, girls leaving home are forced to compete with men. I feel they should stay home, learn how to cook and sew, and become future mothers unless God makes it absolutely crystal clear that they are to pursue a career. In my travels I have met some very fine professional Christian women and missionaries. Otherwise, a woman should fast and pray that God sends a husband, rather than spending dad's $8,000 a year to find one. What, no amens? Dating is harmful. In fact, did you know that dating is not scriptural? Here's why: Partners who are out of the natural protection of families are vulnerable to greater temptation they often can't handle. If you challenge that, then tell me why the pregnancy rate of unmarried Christian girls is climbing so fast? Unlike the 'old days,' colleges, for the most part, are not assuming moral responsibility for students.

"Fourth reason, false value system. The snob system that's created by society, that unless you get that degree, you are less than a person; you get left out of the finer things in life. Did you know that suicide is eight times higher among educated people than uneducated? Did you know that the suicide rate among psychiatrists is four times greater than the people they're trying to help? You know, Jesus didn't say to his disciples, 'Walk with me four years and I'll give you so many credit hours.' He said, 'Wait in Jerusalem and you will receive power.'

"Let me tell you something about the power they received the day of Pentecost. I have received it. I know what it is. I have received the baptism in the Holy Spirit. It is the most far out thing that will ever happen to you when you start to get serious with God. It's not just so you can speak in tongues, and I happen to speak in tongues. You know what it's for? It's for power to further His kingdom. Without it you'll never be as effective in ministry as you would have been had you earnestly sought the Lord for it. Say 'amen' those of you who have received it. (Good response from the audience.)

"To sum it all up, if your education is bringing you into the fullness of Christ, then right on. But are you under conviction that you should be in this school? I mean God has spoken to you, and He has said, 'You'd better go to college, and you're going to be sinning against me unless you go.' Or, are you going for any number of reasons like: draft deferment, finding a husband or wife, sports, to learn how to make money, become a better person, perhaps? None of these are valid reasons. The only valid reason is to be a better disciple for Jesus Christ.

"And whatever you do, don't allow older Christians around you to destroy your vision once you've heard

The Making Of A Prophet

from the Lord. Most older Christians I meet have lost their first love. They witness once a year for the Lord and justify the rest of the year's silence by 'I don't button-hole people, I live my Christian life before them.' They pressure their kids to go to the best schools to assure the best possible financial future instead of encouraging them to trust God more day by day. By example, they teach self security with their big insurance policies, retirement funds and other investments, while most of the effective workers for the kingdom are hurting for finances. Because they are insensitive to the Holy Spirit, they send practically all their missionary money overseas and ignore workers here. The high point of their Christian life is attending church. But you cannot serve Jesus in a church unless you've been called to work there. The only place to serve Him is in the world."

That, basically, was the Wheaton College message. At the very end, a boy jumped up on the stage and told me he had a short leg. I checked it and saw it was less than an inch short. I prayed and it grew out even with the other leg. He announced it to the people filing out, and there was a big silence. But, to our group, it was a confirming sign from the Lord that our message was right on.

That same year, we were asked to speak at Greenville College and later Bryan College, a fundamental school in Dayton, Tennessee, through the efforts of Marve Keener. I repeated the message I gave at Wheaton College and within twenty minutes after finishing, I was asked to leave the Bryan campus. My plane wasn't leaving till that afternoon, so I went to Marve's home and some students came to talk about the Lord and the Holy Spirit baptism. Some were prayed for and healed as a confirming sign from the Lord. Of course, I felt pretty bad about having been kicked off the campus, but God wasn't finished. Around 4:00 in the afternoon, the president called. He was extremely polite.

"Ron, your message in chapel this morning has raised a lot of questions. Some of the students feel strongly that you should come back to tomorrow's chapel. Would you come?" I prayed and talked it over with the students visiting with me and decided to accept. "Lord," I prayed, "you got me down here. You've got to be with me tomorrow. I'm in a well 600-feet deep, and you're the only way out of it."

I slept well that night. The next morning, bright and early, I was back in chapel, ready for whatever came. The awesomeness of the situation made my every breath a prayer to the throne. The man who would ask me the questions was, of course, the speech professor, and he didn't even need a microphone.

My first remarks to the student body were, "You still love me? I love you, and I hope that at the end of forty minutes, you'll still love me, because what really counts is that we have the Lord in common and that we can respect each other's views."

One of the first questions asked me was, "How do you reconcile your extreme views on medicine and education, for example, with such scriptures as Paul's: 'All things are yours. God has given us richly all things to enjoy. Be wise as serpents and harmless as doves, using the world but not abusing it. Your moderation will be known to all men. The Lord is at hand.'"

I answered, "I think that all things are ours and that

The Making Of A Prophet

we need to know that the world system is subject to us and not let it control us. I think that when I have to run to a doctor to get a flu shot, I'm letting that control me. I'm not taking advantage of the promises in scripture that make it very clear I have a certain power that I need to exercise and claim."

Another question was, "Yesterday you laid hands on some people for healing. Doesn't James tell us to call the elders together, anoint them with oil? Please explain your actions."

I answered, "In our church, I am considered an elder. In this body down here, I'm not. But, Mark 16:17 says, 'These signs shall follow them that believe. In my name, they will cast out devils, they shall speak with new tongues, they shall take up serpents, and if they drink any deadly thing it shall not harm them. *They shall lay hands on the sick* and they shall recover.' And so, I accept and claim the promise of God that I can do the same things that Jesus did. He even promised that I'd do greater things than He did."

"All right, then let me ask you this," the professor said. "You have said that men have been influential in your life in many instances--your conversion, the baptism of the Holy Spirit, etc. Do we have a dichotomy here, the Holy Spirit on one hand and man on the other?"

"No. But I think for too long Christians, in their laziness, have listened to others for guidance. The sad thing is that seminaries in this country have turned out men who have mislead flocks. Christians have been fed milk. In fact, it's powdered milk, and we wonder why we have not grown. However, the scriptures make it very clear that if you go to the Bible, the Holy Spirit will teach you all things that you need to know. When you begin to see the truth, you go back to your pastor with your Bible and you say, 'Pastor, it says in this book that healing is for today. But every time you give a message on healing, you talk about Paul's thorn in the flesh, and that we should be satisfied with suffering for Christ. Let's talk about it.'"

Another question was, "You use the word 'scholar' in a derogatory way. What is your definition of scholarship? Do you think Paul and Luke were well trained and keen thinkers? Was Luke not a trained physician?"

I thought a moment, then answered, "If you search the scriptures, I think you'll find that the previous backgrounds of these men were not referred to as being helpful in ministry. As a matter of fact, Paul said very deliberately that he counted his past as dung. He wasn't concerned about all the head knowledge that he had received. 'I preach one thing, Christ, and Christ crucified,' he said. So the fact that these people were trained had nothing to do with what happened after they were converted. What they did by God's power is the issue. I see no admonition by Paul to go to the universities of his day. To the contrary, he said, 'Seek Christ and Christ crucified.'"

After I was finished speaking, the president came up to denounce "extremism in religion." I gave him a big bear-hug. He froze like a ramrod drum major and I know the students loved it.

Interestingly, Bryan College was named after William Jennings Bryan, the attorney in the famous "Monkey Trial" which took place back in the early part of this century. A teacher from Tennessee wanted to change the state law that only allowed the scriptural

The Making Of A Prophet

version of creation to be taught, not Darwin's Theory of Evolution. William Bryan, during the trial, defended a literal translation of scripture. But the question the Bryan College staff was really asking me was, "Don't you take the Bible too literally?" It's ironic that the school was named after a man who wanted to do just that. How times have changed.

Later that year I gave the same message at Judson College, mostly through the work of Cathy Rooney who had been coming to our meetings. A short time after, the school passed a resolution that all future speakers would have to have approved credentials in their theology.

The world says, "Get educated, get smart." The Word says, "Trust in the Lord with all your heart and lean not unto your own understanding, in all your ways acknowledge Him and He shall direct your paths." (Proverbs 3:5)

According to Bill Gothard, a renowned Bible teacher, a survey taken at Michigan State University showed that 85% of all graduating students left school with less faith than when they entered. If you don't send your young people to college as missionaries these days they will return as mission fields! A recent article in the *Washington Times* reveals why.

> For decades, American college campuses have been hotbeds of liberalism and radicalism. And in more recent years, those same campuses essentially were single-handedly responsible for inventing and proliferating the odious doctrine of political correctness. Even by these well-known "standards," however, the campus-wide political-diversity statistics published in the September issue of the *American Enterprise* magazine are

eye-popping.

At Cornell University, the left exceeded the right by a 166-6 margin. In the English department, the left outnumbered the right 35-1. In the history department, it was 29-0. Professors of the left reigned in the political science department, 16-1. In the women's studies department, it was 33-0.

At Harvard University, the collective left/right ratio for the economics, political science and sociology departments was 50-2. At Stanford, the left outnumbered the right by 151-17. At the University of California at San Diego, the ratio was 99-6. At the University of Colorado at Boulder, it was 116-5. Even at the University of Texas at Austin, the left outnumbered the right by 94-15.

For the six universities where a breakdown was provided for journalism departments, the left collectively outnumbered the right 61-6. That lopsided division undoubtedly helps to explain why a 1996 survey by the Freedom Forum and the Roper Center found that 89 percent of Washington-based news-bureau chiefs and congressional correspondents voted for Bill Clinton in 1992 over President Bush, who received 7 percent of the vote.

...For all the incessant talk about the indispensable need for diversity in the student body generated by affirmative action, the utter lack of political diversity among the nation's university faculties speaks volumes about the rampant hypocrisy that pervades America's college campuses.

Some say, "I know all that, that's why I sent my son or daughter to a Christian school." Well, most Christian schools today are poor substitutes for what Jesus taught. They put more emphasis on academic standards than on discipleship. They have substituted theology for kneeology. I believe every school course offered should, as an end result, bring the student a little closer to being a disciple of Jesus. Of course, this is impossible if the school must adhere to state academic requirements in order to be accredited or let the government gain control through grants, which means many subjects unrelated to discipleship must be taught. Jesus said you can't serve two masters. I believe this is why many Christian schools produce so little reproducing fruit, and in the future will lose their identity entirely.

Notice, too, how Jesus taught His men. He didn't lecture over them as today's Christian teachers do, but He took them by the hand and demonstrated in everyday life what He was saying. He didn't just give them head knowledge, but "a way of life." More often, the "way" offered today is equipping one for a secure life rather than emphasizing **F**orsaking **A**ll **I** **T**rust **H**im-- **FAITH**.

FIVE

IN 1972 I WAS ASKED BY HENRY CARLSON of the Full Gospel Businessmen to travel to Sweden with a team of 25 of our young people. When we announced it at our meeting one night, the whole group wanted to go. It blessed me to see so many who were willing to raise their own expenses and make other sacrifices to share their faith on the mission field. It was quite a task deciding who should go. I finally determined that whoever could raise the money and had demonstrated a concern for the lost went, and we met the quota just fine. Two main music groups, "Morning Glory" and "Homeward Bound," plus soloists like Gary Zeleski, would give us change of pace from the preaching Roy Seekins and I would do.

Roy was 23 and had dropped out of Wheaton College. Like so many who had come to us, he was sick of the games Christians play. I met him and his brother, Frank, at a prayer meeting one night. They came home to live with us, and little did I realize, he would marry our second oldest, Vicki, within a year. Another blessing was that three of our oldest, Nick, Vicki, and Rita were eager to go to Sweden too.

Well, we had quite a time there. They split us up

into several groups; the demand for Jesus People was very great. In fourteen days we were in 120 different meetings in schools, streets, and churches. Simultaneously, Roy and I received a message from the Lord that in the future, the church in Sweden would come under great persecution and must stay close to God; that the Pentecostals, especially, should not rely on meetings or feelings for their spiritual life, but should learn the Bible and base their faith on the promises of God.

Unlike America, the schools were open to evangelism. In one school Nick and I went to everything was going along fine until I began to come against immorality. Those who attacked us hardest were the women teachers. We almost felt that they would become physically abusive.

I left there a little depressed. So many people were rejecting God's help for their problems. I went over to another school where I had put Roy Seekins in charge of a team. This particular school was situated on the side of a large quarry filled with water. One of our kids came running up to me. "Ron, you'll never guess what happened! Roy started preaching from Genesis to Revelation. He preached for an hour and when he got finished he said, 'To prove to you that what I'm saying is true, I'm going to show you a miracle. Does anyone here have one limb shorter than another, or a crooked limb, or anything of that nature? One of the girls had a short leg. He prayed for her and her leg grew out immediately, even with the other!"

I learned later that Roy had prayed with 15 kids to receive Christ after they experienced the miracle. I walked over to the edge of the cliff and saw between

The Making Of A Prophet

300 to 400 kids down at the bottom where Roy was baptizing the new converts. I made my way down and Roy let me baptize the last girl.

The newspapers in Sweden picked up that incident by saying that we had come to Sweden to throw 13- and 14-year-old girls into a cesspool. Satan is always trying to wipe out the footprints of God. Christians on the campus retaliated and at least one newspaper printed a retraction. We praised God for the Christians who took a stand.

One of the team members on that trip to Sweden was a boy named Paul Schoenthal. Before the airlift I had been going to the College of DuPage to witness to young people in the cafeteria. I will always be grateful to college administrations for the freedom to speak about the Lord on campuses. At DuPage kids would sit in the cafeteria socializing. We tried to pick out those who sat alone and looked unhappy. I would start out with, "Hi, I'm an evangelist, and I like to talk about God. Would you like to rap a couple of minutes?" Nine out of ten would say, "Sure, why not. I've got nothing else to do."

One Monday morning I saw Paul with his head in his hands and my heart went out to him. He looked on the tough side; he hadn't shaved in a week. I guess I hesitated for a moment. Finally, I sat down and introduced myself. "You look like you could use a miracle in your life."

"Yeah, I could use something," he said.

I said, "Well you know, when I found Jesus four years ago it really changed my life and gave me something to live for."

"Yeah, but how do I find Jesus?"

"You simply ask Him to come into your life. It's like a business contract. You sign on the dotted line and then He signs."

"I never thought of it that way," he said.

"There's a verse you can put your faith into," I said. "It's Revelation 3:20, 'Behold I stand at the door and knock, if anyone hears my voice and opens the door, I will come into him.' That's a promise you can count on. I did it, and it worked. You want to try it?"

He looked at me and wet his lips and said, "Yeah, I want to try it." He prayed out loud and his plea to the Savior really touched me. It wasn't until he went over to the Christian book table and told the Christians what happened that he got a "rush." He began to grin and he hasn't stopped since. Four years later we were overjoyed when he married our daughter, Rita.

It was during this time that I happened to be in a Jewish community on the north side of Chicago. It was a beautiful summer day and the Lord told me to witness to several Jewish kids that were sitting outside of a public school. Since school was out they didn't have too much to do but sit around and smoke reefers. They thought I was a narcotics agent but I said, "Look guys, I'm not a narc. I'm just a guy who loves God and I came to talk to you about Jesus Christ. I want to give you some food for thought." I started to tell them about the materialistic trip that most people are into and that the reason they are unhappy is because they've lived their lives without God. A couple of the boys were really anti-Christ, and after almost getting into a shouting match with them, I said, "I've had it with you guys. I came over to have a conversation with you but all you want to do is act like teeny-boppers. If any of

The Making Of A Prophet

you want to do some serious talking about God, I'll be over in my car. I'll wait for five minutes. You come if you're interested; otherwise, I'm taking off."

I'd never done such a bold thing in my life but it seemed to be right. I climbed in the car and prayed, "Lord, send them over; send the hungry ones over." I looked up. Three of the loudest mouths were walking towards me. They said, "All right, what is this about God?"

I asked, "Are you serious?"

They nodded affirmatively.

I said, "Let's sit down." We sat down on the parkway and I laid a rap on them. I told them how Christ had died for their sins and how he loved them; how He was a Jew like them and that all the apostles were Jews; that to accept Christ didn't mean that you turned away from your Jewry--it meant that you became a completed Jew.

The kid on my left kept saying, "If I only had a sign, if I only had positive proof that God exists, I'd believe."

"It's not a question of believing intellectually," I said. "Believing according to what Christ taught means to totally trust Him and commit your life to Him. If He were sitting here right now and you could reach out and touch Him, would you commit your life to Him? Would you let Him tell you what to do with your life?"

"Well, I don't know if I'm ready for that," he said.

"That's the point," I said. "The Jews in Jesus' time wanted a sign too, but when they got their sign, many walked away from Him because whenever God shows you something, it's usually going to cost you. Once you're sure God exists, then sooner or later you're going to have to make a decision to accept or reject Him."

But the lad kept bugging me, "If I only had a sign, if I only had a sign." Getting a little irritated with him, and more to shut him up than anything, I said, "Does anyone here have a short arm or leg?" Sure enough, the kid sitting opposite me had a short arm. I told him to stick out his arms in front of him and one was about three-quarters of an inch shorter than the other. The kid to my left, the doubter, jumped up and said, "You got your arms goofy," and he tried to pull his shoulders around from behind.

"No, I know. My father owns a clothing store and when I put on a coat the left sleeve is always too long," the kid told him.

"All right, you hold your arms out there and you other guys watch this," I said. I held his hand in the open palm of my left hand, which I always did, rather than grabbing him so that people couldn't accuse me of manipulation.

"Father, in Jesus' name, I pray for this arm, that it might grow out, that your Son may be manifested as Jesus Christ." I no sooner said that, when the arm grew out even with the other.

Their mouths flew open, their eyes bulged. They stuttered and stammered. The kid who had the short arm kept saying, "I don't believe it, I don't believe it!"

"You've just seen God answer prayer," I said. "You had a healing take place. Tomorrow, you go to your father's store and put on one of those coats and tell him about the crazy guy that came to your school and told you that Jesus was the Messiah. Would you do that for me?"

The Making Of A Prophet

"I'll do it. I'll do it," he said. I turned to the boy on my left, and said, "There's your sign, what's your answer?" He didn't say anything; he just looked down.

Those boys were changed when I left that day. I can't say they were converted but some good seeds were planted. So often in evangelism we push to see conversions because of soulish zeal, only to see many fall away. But an evangelist with signs and wonders will always be more effective.

When I first heard about limbs being lengthened it didn't set right with me, I couldn't understand it. I realize now that many people do have a short leg; chiropractors will tell you this. In many cases it puts strain on the lower back. You can't see a cancer healed before your eyes because often that's internal. Most people don't have a blind eye, or crooked fingers, or other physical defects to be miraculously healed. But many do have this problem, so God uses it to prove Himself and to help them.

When I returned from Sweden it seemed like all hell had broken loose in the family and I couldn't get freedom to minister. Satan was obviously trying hard to shut down our ministry. I went through a very dark time then, and it seemed probable the old serpent would have his way. My family was really suffering and I didn't know how to solve some of the emerging problems. My wife began going out with her girlfriends at night and coming in at all hours--that really tore me up. I could not communicate with her. I realize now, that a lot of the problems were caused by my not meeting her needs.

Admittedly, I was quite tied up with the street kids. We had a big drug problem in the towns like Wheaton and West Chicago, Illinois, and I didn't see anyone going out to these young people. I really felt a responsibility to do so, and I felt God wanted me to because He seemed to anoint everything we did.

These were good times because they were times of results. Kids would come to the house seeking help and end up finding Jesus and getting baptized in our lake. We baptized over a thousand young people, sometimes breaking ice with a sledge hammer to do it.

But problems between Gloria and myself were growing steadily worse. One night she and I were having dinner in a restaurant and she opened up. "You have placed the ministry ahead of us. You've turned our home into a church, a training center, a crash pad, and you have never really understood how hard it is for a woman to share her home with the world."

I saw I would have to change. The scriptures make it clear that equally important with reaching kids was my responsibility to meet the needs of my family. The first thing I did was ask "Jesus is Lord" fellowship to find a new meeting place. I began to spend time with Gloria. If she wanted to watch TV, so did I. We seldom went out to eat but because it seemed to mean a lot to her to get off by ourselves, I did it. I put things aside, I put the Jesus people aside, and little by little I was able to divorce myself from the ministry.

We began to have some good times, and gradually were communicating the feelings deep inside. When she saw my honest effort she began to change. She became less independent and things gradually became much better.

The Making Of A Prophet

We couldn't know then that we were rebuilding a relationship that would enable us to get through the toughest next three years of our marriage.

Twenty-five Jesus people from "Jesus is Lord" fellowship in Stockholm, Sweden, ministered in 120 different meetings in schools, malls, and churches over 14 days.

TOP: Ron preaching at at a high school in Sweden.
BOTTOM: Roy Seekins praying for a Swedish student. Her leg was lengthened as a confirming sign of the Gospel.

TOP: Henry Piirainen, our "far out" Swedish interpreter, has faithfully kept in touch down through the years.
BOTTOM: Elder Ken Downey and son, Timothy.

SIX

RHONDA WAS ONLY TWELVE when she began coming home from school acting strangely; but it wasn't until we discovered a letter she had written to a girlfriend that we learned she'd been using drugs. I remember I went into the bedroom and got down on my knees and wept before the Lord. At that moment He never seemed further away. There had been a colossal mistake made in the universe. How could He have ever let this happen? He promised there would be testing, but this?

We tried to reach her but evidently she had been building a wall for months and now it seemed unbreachable. She'd give us her word that she would stop "using" and we would catch her with the stuff. So we began to lose faith in her.

Many nights I sat alone in the dark and tried to understand where we had gone wrong. I always came up with the same answer: being the second youngest in a family of five children she had been lost in the crowd. She never received a lot of attention from me so her basic love needs were rarely met. Having gone through the same thing early in my own life I knew exactly the hurt she must have felt, but strangely, I was powerless to help her now. I would tell her about the Lord and that He could answer all her problems but she couldn't catch hold. She had accepted Christ some years earlier, but like so many kids, never got down to business serving Him. I know now that in those early years of her life, her greatest need was to have her daddy, not Jesus.

She'd try all right. I remember the Jesus concerts she wanted to go to and the people she'd seek out for counsel. After awhile I'd back off talking about the Lord to her but the young people living with us and her brothers and sisters were always talking about Him. It had to have bothered her. According to our Children and Family Welfare Services case worker, Rhonda wanted to follow our lifestyle but couldn't be consistent, so giving up, she sought acceptance from kids in the streets.

Her mother and I would vacillate between committing her completely to God and taking her back again; by yelling at her, or restricting her too much, or not going that extra mile that Jesus would have. I'm sure we hindered God's plan by allowing ourselves to get emotionally involved. We should have prayed ten times more than we did. But you know, it's hard. It's hard to remember that you're only a baby sitter for your children until they can make it on their own. Your feelings keep getting in the way, like the constant fear that any night she's out you're going to get a call from the county morgue saying they've got an overdose case who's ID says she's Rhonda Rendleman.

She and I had a long talk out on our "Jesus path" early in her first year in high school. She wanted help and felt going to West Chicago High where all her

The Making Of A Prophet

doper friends were, was pulling her down. I had a talk with the principal of the school and he made arrangements for home tutoring until she was emotionally stronger. But he needed a confirming letter from a psychiatrist and by the time we found one and had some sessions with him, six weeks had elapsed. In November, 1971, the unbelievable happened.

A police officer came to our door to take her into custody. His explanation was vague but he had a warrant and I had to let her go. She and I were home alone when it happened. We stood in the hall while the cop waited outside and I took her in my arms and prayed, "God, I don't know what's going on here, but I trust you to look after her and keep her safe..."

I watched the car pull away and I saw her looking back as long as she could and I wondered if she were crying too. I sat in an empty house all afternoon seeking God and I think that was the first time I received the thought that was to come to me many times later in life: *Your life is a book with many chapters and the last chapter has yet to be written, so don't prejudge the book.*

According to the official records Rhonda was taken into custody because she was truant from school, a drug user needing additional supervision that we, supposedly, were unable to give her. Evidently, she wanted complete freedom and was sure a foster home was the answer. She had gone to a local juvenile office a few days before the arrest. She was only thirteen and she never lived at home for any length of time after that.

There was a court hearing during which her mother

and I were asked to testify. I was beginning to recover from the shock of having her yanked out of our home and started to unload on the court. The judge stopped me and the assistant district attorney, with a slight smirk, asked, "Have you ever told your daughter to repent?"

I thought a moment and said, "If you're asking me if I ever asked my daughter to change her ways, you're darn tootin' I have." As a matter of fact, I don't think I ever did use the word "repent" to her.

Well, she got her wish. The court said she "was a neglected minor, whose behavior was injurious to her welfare," and placed her in a foster home. Very official sounding and the "neglected" part was very untrue and a very hard thing to hear, especially when you know how much you love.

Certain communist members of Congress from time-to-time have tried to introduce legislation known as the Child and Family Service Act. It takes the responsibility of the parents to raise their children and gives it to the government. The following excerpts are taken from a congressional record:

> What is at issue is whether the parent shall continue to have the right to form the character of the children or whether the state, with all its power and magnitude, shall be given the decisive tools and technique for forming the young lives of the children of this country.
>
> As a matter of the child's right, the government shall exert control over the family because we have recognized the child is not the care of the parents but the care of the state. We recognize further that not parental, but communal forms of upbringing have an unquestionable superiority over all other forms. Furthermore, there is a serious question that maybe we

cannot trust the family to prepare young children in this country for this new kind of world which is emerging.

In the Charter of Children's Rights of the National Council of Civil Liberties which is a part of this proposal there is the following statement:

"Children have the right to protection from any excessive claims made on them by their parents or authority. The question was asked, by way of example, what do you mean by the fact "excessive claim"? And the example was given, "If the mother or father asks the child to take the garbage out and the child doesn't want to, the parents have no right to insist on it." A similar proposal is in the United Nations Convention on the rights of the child and unless God intervenes, true to form, our Congress will sign on to this bit of madness. As a nation, we long ago decided we could solve life's problems better than our Creator. And suddenly, the words of the Savior come blazing back:

"O America, America (Jerusalem, Jerusalem)... how often I wanted to gather your children together just as a hen gathers her brood under her wings, and you would not have it! Behold, your house is left to you desolate..." (Luke 13:34,35)

The court let Rhonda come home after three months and for awhile things were great. But a few months later, without warning, Rhonda ran away from her home. She later wrote about it.

> One night, after I'd been home awhile, I got too stoned with a friend and never made it home that night. The next morning I couldn't think of an excuse. I was tired of making excuses.
>
> I left town about six a.m. The sun was just coming up as I stood on the nearest highway. I didn't think too

much about where I was headed, I just knew I couldn't stay.

A group of college kids picked me up on their way back to school in Madison, Wisconsin. I pretended to be on my way to visit a friend there. They dropped me off at the main office where I found a whole bunch of people standing around a big bulletin board. On it were several small cards made out by students looking for rides, or riders to share with gas and driving on their trips home. Next to me stood a tall blond girl. She noticed me looking at her and smiled.

"Are you looking for a ride too?" she asked.

"Sort of, why?" I answered.

"Because," she said, "if you can't share with gas you may as well forget it."

"Well, I guess I'm not looking for a ride around here then," I said, and walked out the door. When I got out to the road I put out my thumb, and it wasn't but a minute later that she came running out.

"My name is Lisa, need any company?" she smiled as she stuck out her thumb too. She knew she was welcome.

She looked pretty thin and she slept a lot the first day we were together. I just figured she'd had it hard. We got along pretty good and it was nice to have someone to talk to. I just couldn't figure out why she never woke up from the daze she was in when I met her.

Then one afternoon I figured it out. We'd caught a ride with a guy in a fancy car with a glove compartment full of dope. I thought he was a little careless, but Lisa hit it off pretty well with him. Before we got out, she sweet-talked him out of nearly all the downers he had. She ate them like candy. I couldn't see getting down like that on the road, but she was older than I was and I didn't figure she'd listen anyway.

The Making Of A Prophet

About a week passed. Lisa lost her appetite and was getting sick. We were somewhere in southern Indiana and some trucker had let us off in the middle of nowhere right before a weight station. He was afraid to get busted with us because the place was swarming with state patrol. We were seen and picked up for walking on a "no pedestrian" freeway. Three days later, they sent Lisa to some drug rehabilitation place, and me on a bus to Chicago.

I waited for two hours in Chicago but no one showed to meet me. I learned later the Indiana cops had dropped the ball. I thought of calling, and even stayed around Chicago for a week thinking about it. I was afraid to call the police and give myself up because they would probably put me in jail, and if I called my parents, my mom would start crying on the phone, and I couldn't handle that.

I decided to go back down south. I gathered enough food and clothes for the trip and headed on the same highway through the same towns. I didn't like sleeping outside alone if I didn't have to, so I usually found the nearest town at night. It wasn't any hassle in town to find some place to stay. People were always friendly.

The further I got away from home, the safer I thought I'd be. I couldn't tell anyone that I was a runaway because they wouldn't want to be caught with me, so I made up all kinds of stories. Truckers gave me money for food, or some would just buy me food. Most of them believed that females hitching sold their bodies, but I made it clear that I didn't.

One afternoon I was standing on a ramp somewhere in southern Louisiana, I didn't see any "no hitchhiking" sign, but the policeman claimed that there was one. I didn't argue very long.

It was the same old story. He asked me for identification, suspected that it was invalid, and took me in to run a check. He found out about the Illinois warrant so it was all over for me.

They called my parents first, who said they'd notify the police in my home town. My ma decided that instead of letting the police goof again she'd come for me herself.

I was sitting in a small Louisiana jail eating beans and coffee when she showed with my brother. She looked tired and worn. My heart ached with guilt. I thought of running, but how could I run after she'd come so many miles for me.

It's impossible to describe the feeling that grips you when you think of your daughter being out there at the mercy of someone who may harm her. It hurts, too, to know she doesn't want to live with you any longer and you do a lot of heavy soul searching. And you begin to understand what faith is all about. *Believing* in something is no longer adequate. Now *complete trust* in the Savior to intervene and straighten out the whole mess is the only way to get any peace of mind. Gloria and I never stopped praying for her and gradually a confidence settled over us that enabled us to go on living and filling the needs of those around us.

I'll never forget the night mom returned with Rhonda. As she walked slowly up the driveway, she was the sorriest-looking hippy in the world. Blue jean bell bottoms dragged through mud, hair matted, her face haggard, she looked much older. She managed a smile and gave me a big hug and said she was sorry for causing so much hassle. I was mad and glad to see her at the same time, but I knew she needed to be comforted more than anything so I just tried to be more glad than mad.

Being a ward of the court meant she had to turn

The Making Of A Prophet

herself in, so she agreed to. We drove her to the youth home the next day and had another tearful goodbye. She spent an unbelievable three months locked up there while the court decided what to do.

We were allowed to see her only once a week so letters became our lifeline to each other. As we wept over each expression received, whether a poem, or mood piece, or just a note--her efforts to tear down her part of the wall became more evident. I've saved some of those that were the most expressive.

>
> Dear Pa--
> you see, it goes on and I'm so tired.
> I know I love you...
> but I can't come to changing for you
> Please, Daddy, I ain't no bum
> or fried mind,
> or idiot being tossed about.
> I can see me flying backwards, facing you,
> and crying heavy.
> Both of us that way.
> I try to say,
> you try to relate,
> But isn't it what we feel,
> not what we say?
> I don't want to be a junkie,
> or totally lost,
> without owning my body,
> don't tell me that's where I'm headed.
> But words, as you know, don't make it.
> No matter what you did,
> It didn't give me the right to
> build the other half of the wall.
> Oh, Dad, I want you to help me.
> I love you.

Ron Rendleman

I'm crying. Yes I'm crying.
And I just don't know how it's going to end
I'm thinking back it's a long time that,
I cussed my daddy down.
They were bad evil nights
When I realized what I'd done, it was way too
late, too late for words and I'm crying--
sometimes we hurt each other so bad.
Nobody to turn to, no going back
No such thing as God for me now.
No more to rap to him
No more to let him know.
All I can do is break down in tears
I'm crying and wondering
Where am I now because of what I did.
I just don't know and I'm crying
It was a long time ago
But the pain is not over.
And I remember,
How we shared a love, a long time ago.

Dear Dad,

I'm really in a pretty good mood, but worried about the hearing tomorrow. I have to explain something.

Sometimes when I'm talking to you, as you know. I get really defensive. But more than that, I feel like you are in every little thing I do. Like I don't think you realize the extent of some of the things I was into. And I don't intend to tell you in detail. But for once. I'm asking for help, in one way that you understand kids.

It's so hard to explain. I feel I should of learned to rap to you, and not cop out so much, and blame it all on you, but then I gave up, and started really enjoying tripping and playing games. Coming home, Satan is gonna fight Jesus again.

The Making Of A Prophet

I became brainwashed, thinking that I had to live up to your way of life, standards etc. It's a good cop out isn't it? Whether or not you have hang-ups, or really did force my head into corners or not, is not the issue. I can't use that to completely foul up my life. I'm on the road of finding out.

The intensity is till there, but I've been training myself not to remember those bummer trips and arguments. I'm gonna get my life together, and have to quit blowing things out of proportion about what you say to me.

Some of the things you say to me I will still reject, or do the opposite of, because of this tension between us. It took a lot to build, it'll take a lot to break it down.

You've got to understand--after going through all these hassles, how hard it is to hear someone say, "Forget it, I know what I'm talking about, I'm your father and God says...," it's a bummer trip, and that's when I rebel.

You see, I've got a lot more up in my head than you think, but you think I'm immature and out to impress or find a freak with dope. All satanic attitudes in your eyes. When really what I'm rebelling for is a real value, (probably the same as yours). It looks like I'm making a gigantic issue over seeing my friends, or being "hip." It's a lot more involved than that. Try to see it. In the past you wouldn't understand, and then I wouldn't understand anymore, then I'd come back here and fantasize you, miles away with a string hanging to my mind, then all the Jesus freaks having the advantage over me, praying for me and my own real feelings would be hidden under a mask of some kind.

Can you understand? If you do, it would take a two-year long burden off my head, and break down the thickest wall of all. Ask my wizard, (psychiatrist), about it and see what she says.

Write back, and please leave Jesus off in the distance at least for awhile. He is distorted in my mind and I'm trying to straighten it out. That's why I asked not to see you before. But that was also a cop out - cuz I'm gonna work it out once and for all. Using a straight head, and not stopping till it's done.

I love you, Rhonda

Dear Ma & Pa,

I had to get out of there, away from those kids. They were good enough to let me alone in my cell for awhile. They even let me have a pencil and paper in here. I think they trust me by now--that's good. Those kids, they were trying to have a group discussion on some serious thought-provoking ideas. But it's all a joke to everyone. They sit and laugh and joke and ignored the meaning of the whole discussion.

They get put in here, to get better, but do the same things over again--only worse. Why can't they sit down and realize some things. Stop messing around for 15 minutes and think. I felt like grabbing them and saying, "Quit it and change a little for someone else, he knows, he's gone through it--listen to him and respect him, put down that joint a minute." Oh, it's so hard to explain.

I feel myself turning into part of what I hate. I can see why they do some of these things like locking a kid up to stop him from doing things like killing himself. But yet, I could never cold heartedly lock someone up, because you can get through to him, and it's not by playing "wise man of the year." Maybe you've lived longer and know a lot more than we do, but still things have to be experienced. Morals between generations are different.

I have learned some things. Most kids are just

The Making Of A Prophet

screwed up and their heads are on backwards and are rebellious. But can't you see this isn't me?

I want to respect you, take your advice and love you. That's the hassle I have. While I'm here I intend to straighten some things out. I don't disagree with many things that my parents say, but I don't like them pushed on me, cuz I've got a strong head, and nobody is going to change it unless I want it changed. And I do. I want to be able to find enough out of life so I don't find pleasure out of getting high--not because I feel it's bad or harmful but because it causes dishonesty and hurts those you love. Don't you think that that is a better reason for quitting than harm to yourself?

I get so confused 'cuz I'm only 14, and a lot of things I don't know yet but I'll learn. I like to please authority sometimes to show them that I can think. I'm embarrassed to be here, having to be locked up in with some kids that are plain dumb, defending the "cool hippie trip" in which I wouldn't condone nor cut down. Instead of being here I feel I should be on the staff trying to show these kids that they're ruining their whole lives for something they aren't even sure they want in the first place. I want to do things but then I just don't know. I think I'm going to try my hardest to make myself look for the worthwhile things in this life--and God? Where is He? I wish I knew, maybe He would understand.

Love, Rhonda

Ron Rendleman

Remember my good-looking old man,
standing proud, blue jeans and leather vest?
Hands on hips, shades,
and a smile on his face
look so hep.
Daddy, you've got such a good head,
"Far out man, it's a heavy trip," he explains to the crowd
The Bible is under his arm
Daddy, please put it down--
Bible, obligations, converts and all.
Look at me, I need you.
I'm not into your trip. You persist,
And I boogie away.
Now in the house of detention
I sit--waiting for I dunno what--
I am me, condemned to hell, whatever you say,
But it's still me--do you still care?
Me as me,
rebelling,
your little doped-up kid,
it's still me.
I love you, do you still love me?
I overlook your ignorance of me,
And your persistence on my soul
Can you do the same for me?
I am sorry.
Sometimes I must cry out loud.
I am lonely.

The Making Of A Prophet

Traveling...
As so many things must pass,
so must you,
I perceive
And when you're young and searching,
things seem to pass
so quickly.
Spaces and times,
got so many memories
on my mind.
Spaces.
So many bewildered faces.
Lost.
Being tossed,
and passed.
The same way you were passed.
It all happens so fast.
Experiences with passing people,
Making friends out of strangers,
meeting
sharing a day,
maybe two,
or more.
Then being passed on,
by life,
stopping never for a breath,
not even for strife.

Ron Rendleman

THE LONELY MAN

I saw a lonely man today, he must have been lonely. Not many happy people sit on the side of the road staring at the patterns in the snow. His hair was gray and long, the same length of his white beard. His clothes looked worked over--paint stained, covered with patches. My friends and I sat in a car across the road watching him. They laughed at him, making jokes about the wine bottle in his hand. It was nearly midnight, the streets were deserted except for him, clearly seen under the light. His face looked so tired, worn out. He was so very lonely.

Someone handed me a can of beer, the third case for us that night. The smell of beer and pot flooded every inch of the car; Steve Miller screeched through the speakers. And everyone laughed at this old drunk passing out in the snow.

Then something caught my attention. A friend sitting next to me wasn't laughing. His hair was long, his jeans faded, the same lonely look on his face. He held a joint to his lips, slowly toking, staring at the man in the snow. He glanced at me, and quickly looked away. He stared at his feet and spoke softly. The noise was so loud I bent down low to hear him.

"I better go get my old man," he said. He stumbled out of the car and over to the man. He tried to pick him up, but the two were too drunk to get anything accomplished. The rest of the people in the car had all stopped laughing, surprised at the behavior of their friend.

"It's his Pa," I said, and got out of the car and helped pick him up. When the two were on their feet, I jumped back in the car.

We watched them stagger down the street, arm in arm. "Let's go get some more beer, huh?" someone broke the silence. Drunk and laughing, they turned up the music and we peeled off.

The Making Of A Prophet

After one of our court hearings I was particularly despondent and longing to have our daughter home again. I wrote:

Dear Rhonda,

You've been on my mind much lately--how you're kept there, and we're here and how you must feel being held. When I went to Onarga Military School I think I was the loneliest guy in the world, till I learned self preservation. It's easy to learn, just pull back into your shell like a turtle so that no one can ever hurt you again. Only thing wrong about that is that it's hard to come out of the shell and be a normal person again, very hard. There are better ways and I think you're finding them.

Anyway, getting back to the house, things are definitely changing. The Lord seems to be telling me that the ministry will change. I have lost my taste for concerts, etc. I still love the kids but something different will take place. Moses spent 40 years in the desert before God really began to use him. I've been a Christian six years and have been active most of that time. Perhaps God wants me to be inactive to learn more of Him. Already He has shown me much about love and how rare it is, like fine gold dust. It is the finest of all human traits and anything that takes away from it is wrong. But it isn't all that easy. I've got to work at it. I never got a lot of love when I was a kid so sometimes it's hard to show people that I really care about them and really love them. Love is best shown by action, not by word. Like the court day last week. What a bummer. All that phony politeness while my daughter is being taken off for a year. I wanted to scream at them that they didn't have to do any of it, that you should come home now, that this time would be different.

Ron Rendleman

Yet I knew, really, that it was best that we be parted for a little while longer. Perhaps, so that we can appreciate each other even more. That's what separation does to people, you know. It's going to be good, someday. You'll see. Better close for now. Love ya.

Pa

Dear Pa,

I just got your letter not more than five minutes ago, can't help the tears, you and Ma, the words, so honest. I know what you were feeling in court, I knew you could sense it, the phony politeness, you not even getting to say a word. It's hard for me to write this now, can't see anything. I feel so sad, not even really sad, just spaced, I can't explain it--I'm so sorry, I really am. For the first time in a long time I can feel the simpleness of love communicated from you to me, without anything else I realize you have feelings, deep emotional ones, only it's hard for you to say it, maybe 'cuz I don't even give you a chance, or I just won't listen. I really feel it deeply now, so intense and it hurts, I feel so bad. If only my writing was half way developed I would explain how I feel.

I can see what you felt, wanting to scream out in anger, hurting quietly, their phony plastic ways overwhelming the whole situation.

There sits me and you dressed in long clean white robes, in the woods of Paradise - laughing - loving - enjoying what is pure and beautiful in God. Can it be?

Yes, Pa-Pa it will be good someday - mighty good indeed. But I do agree it will take time and we should be separated a little time longer. But as long as I have this letter to stand on it's a fantastic motivation, never read a letter so many times in my life (It's your letter to me I'm speaking about)...

Rhonda

The Making Of A Prophet

That day in court we mention in our letters was really something. We sat in the judge's chambers in private session and heard all the legal jargon and I couldn't hold back the tears. We wanted to be together as a family so badly--we had been through enough hurt.

Though the social worker recommended returning her home, the judge thought differently. The social worker saw us changing and willing to bend, unlike so many families she had dealt with where a power struggle begins to emerge. "Whose going to win" becomes the name of the gruesome game.

She told me recently she felt all along we would make it because we had a lot invested in each other. She thought I should back off Rhonda more. But how do you back off a fourteen year old, even if she does talk and write like an adult? Ironically, Rhonda believed in all the same things I did, to a point. She would defend me to her counselors, even talk about Jesus as an answer to some of the locked up kids' problems. Mike Fick, on staff of the youth home, was so impressed with Rhonda's ideas that he decided to commit his life to Christ and remarry his wife.

As much as I hated to admit it, she was so much like me it was scary. I could see me in her when I was her age. But one thing was sure. Through the whole horrible nightmare we discovered we really loved one another. And that's when that wall began to crumble. So many times when parents say to their child, "I love you" what they really mean is, "If you do as I say, think like I want you to, conform to my standards, then I'll love you." That's conditional, and not real love. We found we could love her for herself, but hate the wrong actions. The hardest thing for me to do was not to soften so much that I would forget my own principles and not take a stand when I should. She would tell her friends "her Pa really had his head together." Later, I learned the court psychologist saw me as a dominant and religiously demanding and too inflexible, all of which was probably true. But what got me was that she never even met me.

There were several key issues I began to understand. For one thing Rhonda would have to find her own path to God. My lifestyle, my dreams for her, even my morals could not be superimposed on her. She had a zest to live, to experience, to get burned even, if need be.

This is what the kids are saying most often to us. Because of our accelerated times, youth start sowing wild oats at a much earlier age. All a parent can hope to do is teach them while they're young "the way they should go." If the foundation is well laid they will eventually return to it even though they must go through some rough years. I saw a girl scout poster one time that said, "The time to worry about an eighteen year old is when she's eight." It should be much earlier, really.

Well, we'd been through a lot as a family and very soon the great ordeal was about to end.

SEVEN

LARRY WAS 23 when he started coming around. He was very quiet and polite, and of course, had long hair. We thought he was too old for Rhonda who had just turned 15 but it wasn't long before there was talk of marriage.

One gigantic obstacle stood in the way. Rhonda, who had been living in foster homes with an occasional visit to our home, was still a ward of the court. We asked for a hearing but because of her track record it was highly improbable that the judge, who she had appeared before so many times, would suddenly give her complete liberty to marry and move out of the state. Larry went to the hearing with us.

We needed a miracle. We prayed that the Lord would intervene, and sure enough, a miracle happened! A new judge was appointed to the case. Our case worker, Karen Martin, was positive the old judge would have ruled thumbs down. Martin wrote a very persuasive report and I really believe that it helped a lot. Rhonda received her "freedom papers" and a new life. We drove home from the court shouting and praising the Lord every mile of the way. When the car grew quiet for a moment Rhonda leaned over from the back seat and said softly, "Dad, would you marry us?"

I'm not going to even try and describe how I felt at that moment. I think she must have known what it would mean to me, especially after all we'd been through. Previously, I had gone to Henry Carlson of the Full Gospel Businessmen, who had taken our team of Jesus people on the Swedish air lift, and asked him if his church would consider ordaining me as a minister. Let me say quickly--man cannot give another man a ministry, only God can. I wasn't looking for man's approval for a ministry that had already been proven to be of God many times over, but with a formal ordination came a license that allowed me to get into intensive care wards, prisons, and yes, to marry people.

He agreed and on September 9, 1973, I was ordained at Chicago's Faith Tabernacle. Eleven days later, before a small group of Rhonda's friends and relatives, I tied the knot in our living room. The next day we took the kids to O'Hare for their flight to Seattle where Larry had been living and working at a good pay rate. And as I watched the plane taxi off I felt greatly relieved and thankful to God that He had stepped in and helped us. *I would miss her much.* God had done so many things so fast that it was impossible to make sense out of it all.

Sometime later, Rhonda sat down one day and wrote about her new life in Washington.

> I sat on the plane watching my parents waving from the airport. For the first time I cried *leaving* home. They had done so much for me, and now I was finally leaving with their blessing.
>
> We lived in Vancouver, Washington, where I met Larry's relatives and friends. We were very happy even

TOP: Rhonda and Larry White on their wedding day.
BOTTOM: Jesus People marching in downtown Chicago.

The Making Of A Prophet

though I was suddenly in a different social world. All our friends were married and had kids. When I became pregnant I began to realize that I couldn't be an irresponsible kid anymore. I was a woman, and going to give birth to a child.

I finally gave birth to the most far out baby alive, Jason Uriah White. I had a natural childbirth with Larry at my side, and it was really a fantastic experience. As I rubbed the soft head of my infant I remembered all the times when I was hitting up speed. He was so perfect and I didn't deserve him.

As time went on we put together a good relationship with no major hassles. Larry was really precious to me. I couldn't imagine loving another. I sometimes wondered if we would turn out like most of our friends-- hating each other after a few years of marriage. They all swore we would. As far as drugs went, we didn't do much of anything except smoke pot or do speed occasionally.

When Jason was about three months old, Larry lost his job and we had to go on welfare. I told my sister, Vicki, about it who lived in Seattle and her husband, Roy Seekins, offered him a job painting. We moved up to Seattle and lived next door to them. They had been married for awhile, but weren't like our other friends. They didn't cuss at each other and cut each other down. Vicki didn't worry about Roy running around on her. I wondered what it was that made them so tight.

We liked them a lot but they were Jesus people and we thought they wasted their lives on Bible studies and a myth about Jesus Christ. They spoke of His love and grace that could set people free. Larry never heard anything like this, but I had heard it since I was eight. I couldn't understand how a God that never seemed to be around would have anything to do with my life. I was happy enough and didn't want any changes. Since

Ron Rendleman

I had Larry and Jason I'd discovered a real reason for living. I never before noticed the seasons of the year changing or the sparkle in a child's eyes. I had enough to keep me busy in the real world and neither Larry or I wanted to explore another.

One day Larry came home for lunch. He found me sleeping with Jason by my side. He shook me excitedly. "Baby, I gotta talk to ya," he whispered.

I woke up in a daze rubbing my eyes.

"Would you follow me in any kind of life I chose?" he asked. What a silly question, I thought. "Of course honey, what's up?"

"He's real," Larry looked me close in the eyes. "God is real!"

I looked at him for a long time. Just an hour ago he believed that God was dead and buried, now everything had changed. He went on to tell me about how he'd been talking to Roy and then went for a walk to pray.

"There's only two says to go, babe," he explained, "two roads to walk on. I just wanna be on the right one."

There was a love in him that poured over on me. He ran around the house throwing out our pot and speed, smiling all the time. "I don't need this stuff honey, Jesus is all I need."

I didn't understand. We sat down to lunch and Larry bowed his head to pray for the second time in his life. "God," he said, "please let her see it too, thank you for saving me."

I sat staring at him. He ate, kissed me and ran off back to work. What is it that I don't see? I thought about it most of the day. That night we sat outside under the stars. Larry talked a long time about the peace he had in giving his life to Jesus. I laid on my back and listened.

"...God is love and peace," he said, "the Creator of it

The Making Of A Prophet

all." We lay there in silence thinking about creation. Then it clicked. I'd known it so long, but it finally became real to me. "We are God's creations," I said aloud. "He made us to be His friends, He gave us the rivers and trees and every stream...it was a natural thing but we blew it right from the beginning. God created us to live, but we chose to die. That's why He had His Son die. He wants us to live!" It wasn't by chance that I married Larry or gave birth to his baby. Larry took my hand. I said a simple prayer surrendering my life to Jesus. He became real to me then. Not in a gust of wind, or lightening from the sky, but a simple realization that He was by my side and in every living thing.

Rhonda gave birth to two more children, Nathan and Caprice, and hopefully she will never lose her determination to experience life fully (destructive habits excluded of course).

But it's all over now. The worry, the turmoil, the strife have lost their bite and are mere shadows. Once we thought it would go on forever but peace finally did come. We sit now, my wife and I, in the autumn evenings and watch red leaves swirling, and wonder how she's doing. She and Larry finally went separate ways mostly because Larry drifted from his faith and today she lives in Vermont with her new husband, Jerry Dixon.

Some who know our family have asked what all this taught us. It's difficult to relate, because most of the work was done to our souls. We learned we could endure a lot more than we thought. Though Satan did succeed in all but shutting down a ministry that had influenced thousands of lives, God took his attack and used it to burn the dross off my inner man. I learned how to minister to others when I was hurting. I learned that weakness, despised so by man, is highly regarded by God. So many Christians must be held by the hand in their walk with God. Suffering helped me to see that.

Gloria has changed too. She's less apt to hold things in, to pout when she's hurt. The creativity in her began to evolve from creating numerous handcrafts to an accomplished oil paint artist and teacher. I used to think Rhonda was just a rebel without a cause. Now I know she had a cause. Of course, one might ask, "But why didn't the other children rebel?" They may have inwardly, a little, but I believe when they saw how we were hurting with Rhonda, they could never add to it. They were a great help during those years.

As I reflect on those dark times now I'm reminded that a real turning point in Rhonda's attitude occurred, when one night while praying, I received a strong thought to ask her forgiveness for not being there for her when she was very young--by being too busy with self interest, or later, the ministry. It's almost mysterious, but it seems when we ask forgiveness something is released, a healing balm that begins to soothe deep wounds in the one we've wronged. And, interestingly, the wronged person, if he or she is totally honest, can no longer blame the offender for all the problems between them and has to look inside and accept responsibility for his or her wrong actions. That's exactly what happened with Rhonda.

What would I say to someone who may be going through a battle--whether it's an alcoholic spouse or a runaway teen? Just hang on. If you're not a Christian, become one. God's peace and love can make all the

The Making Of A Prophet

difference between going under or getting the victory. If you are a Christian you need to be reminded that all things work together for good for those who love God, that nothing, absolutely nothing, happens to you without God's permission. So learn to thank Him for the bleak times as well as the bright. Prayer is the magic word--not psychiatry, not Ann Landers, not your daily horoscope. Prayer with sin out of the way is a hotline to the throne itself. Then trust. Sit back and wait patiently. You may not understand but you do need to hold His hand.

As a parent, remember you're only a baby sitter for the number one Father. Do what you think best for your child, then let go. You can provoke a child to rebellion by over control. Give him room to breathe, a chance to make a mistake or two. Deal with a young person's conscience, not his emotions. Remember that rebellion many times stems from a wounded spirit--wounded by someone we love.

I guarantee if you don't get mad at God through your ordeal, you'll learn much about love. It comes in different sizes and shapes, the best is sacrificial. To love, when there's no guarantee of getting your own back scratched, or getting sympathy when you're hurting, that's what Jesus is all about. Some of us do it easier than others. Some of us have to suffer first. Just remember your life is a book and it's not over till the last chapter is written. So don't prejudge the book.

Rhonda, all "growed up" and focused now, became the owner of J.I.L. Limousine Company.

EIGHT

IN THE NEXT COUPLE OF YEARS all our children married and left home except Roy, our retarded son, who remained to attend special schools and cheerfully help out with household chores. Divorced from youth ministry, I began to consider using my talents as a writer to help further God's kingdom.

The first book published was *Tears for a King*, a story about black slavery. After being rejected by 17 publishers over several years, Successful Living bought the story for their inspirational book racks in retail stores around the country. Almost immediately, I began getting letters from Blacks thanking me for my efforts. One 13-year-old girl wrote: "...I didn't know a white man could write so good about a black man's problems...I give you an "A." But I need to ask a favor. Could you help me write a book report?"

I wrote back, "Thanks for the hearts and flowers, but if I help you with your book report, how will you ever learn how to write well enough to inspire a white man someday?"

Next I wrote *Disciple in Blue Suede Shoes*, about Carl Perkins, the country singer. I flew down to Jackson Tennessee, I believe it was in 1976, to interview

The Rendleman kids. Except for Roy, all married now with their own families. Top to bottom: Nick, the oldest, then Vicki, Rita, Rhonda, and Roy.

Dad and Mom, Roy and Angeline Rendleman, now deceased, fervently served the Lord in their later years. Standing with Ron, kid sister, Jeannine Stavlo, who, with husband, Dale, have dedicated their lives and their family to service for the Kingdom.

him and came away deeply moved by his story. He told me how he, Johnny Cash, and Elvis Presley had all begun their careers about the same time and how all three had succumbed to habits of dope or booze. Cash was the first to go clean and "walk the line" after he had prayed to Christ for help. Immediately he began working on Carl.

It was in San Diego, California, where it began for Carl. Twelve thousand fans were rhythmically clapping and yelling impatiently for the Johnny Cash concert to begin. Carl usually opened the show with "Blue Suede Shoes," but this night he was "drunker than a skunk." For years he had been able to perform under the influence--it took away stage jitters, and gave him a little "spice," as he put it. Somehow, with Cash's help, he got through his opening segment and back to their bus where he passed out. As he tells it:

> The next morning I awoke in the back of Johnny's bus, deathly sick and painfully aware of the fool I had made of myself the night before. Dimly I could make out the sounds of laughter outside somewhere. June Carter and John were up front. June must have heard me moaning.
>
> "How you feelin', Carl?" she asked, leaning over me.
>
> "Not so good. I feel like dying."
>
> "Carl, John wanted to die too. But look at him now. Why don't you do what he did. Call on God. He'll help you."
>
> "I don't deserve to live," I cried. "I ought to die. God cain't love me anymore."
>
> "Oh, yes He does," she said. "You talk to Him. John and I'll let you be. When you feel up to it, come join us and the others. We're fixin' to have a picnic. John drove us to a nice spot by the ocean."

The Making Of A Prophet

I lay there alone for a long time in a stupor. Once I tried to get up but couldn't--a forceful hand seemed to shove me down. I was sick to my stomach, my head was spinning, and I was sure fuzzy, big-eyed bugs were crawling all over me. I'd never experienced such horror before. I was scared! Was I dying? I started praying aloud. "Lord, I don't have the right to ask You to let me live, but, Lord, if I'm dying, let me live long enough to get home to see Val and my little kids. Let them see me sober, but don't let me die here, like this."

After awhile I began to feel a little better. I looked around and spotted my brown tote bag on the floor. I knew what was in that tote bag. I reached over for it and found my nearly full pint of whiskey from the night before. I was lifting the bottle to my lips when a very real, but inaudible voice interrupted me. *Carl, you asked Me to let you make it home, but if you take one drink you'll never see your family again.* I knew who was speaking. It was the One I had ignored most of my life. I couldn't risk ignoring Him any longer. I put the cap back on the bottle, struggled to my feet, and groped my way through the bus. Just when I got to the front, John climbed in.

"Are you still drinking, Carl?" he asked, looking at the bottle I was starting to put in my hip pocket.

"No, John," I answered. "I've decided that if I can walk off this bus, I'm going to throw this bottle away."

"Come on, I'll help you," he said.

"No, I'm going to do it myself," I said. "If you can do it, so can I. He's my God too."

Somehow, I made it outside. I was standing on a blazing white beach. Lying vast and magnificent before me was the Pacific Ocean. Members of the group were swimming, playing, having a great time. I went off by myself to a secluded place down near the water, looked out across that ocean, a breathtaking testimony to God's handiwork, and thought about the commitment I had made a year earlier on Easter Sunday. My wife, Val, and I and the kids were in our church, the Bemis Methodist Church in Jackson, Tennessee. The preacher gave an invitation for us to give our lives to God. Val, my son Stan, and my daughter, Debbie, stood up and waited for me to let them by. I let them out and watched them walk that aisle, and then God spoke to me. *Carl, you come, too. I want you to confess before everyone in this church that you believe in Me. You know you do.*

For years I had been staggering around in life, a nominal Christian, gaining a step and falling back two, a slave to the bottle, half a husband, half a father, and I knew it was because I was serving the wrong lord. I started to break out in perspiration. My heart was pounding. I did believe in Jesus Christ, but the lord I had been serving was blocking the way out of that pew. But I would not be stopped. Not this time. I got out into the aisle and almost ran to join my family who were on their knees down at the front of the church.

And now as I stood on that California beach, God reminded me of that vow. I reached into my back pocket and pulled out the bottle and studied it. After a moment I dropped to my knees.

"Lord, I let You down. I told You I'd never drink again. I'm gonna' have to have You in order not to. I know I can't do this all by myself. Help me, Lord." As I stood up and threw that devil's brew far out into the ocean, I knew I had broken his power in my life and great joy swept over me.

I sat down on the warm sand and watched sea gulls diving into the surf. A cool ocean breeze caressed my face, the sun warmed my back, and I felt like I was in heaven. I can't describe the strength that seemed to be

The Making Of A Prophet

lifting me high--as high as the gulls circling overhead.

I lay on my back and let the sun bore into my face and chest. And then the first doubts came. Doubts that just as all the other times, I would fail this time too. Many a night during the years I was with John, he and I would sit in back of his motor home after a show-- him with his pills and beer, me with my fifth of bourbon. We'd talk about our lives, our dreams, our failings, and always we'd end up misty eyed talking about God. Neither of us wanted to lean on crippling habits, but we couldn't seem to face daily life without them. When I first started drinking as a teen, I never dreamed I'd become addicted--no one does, I guess, but it got so bad that I'd put away a fifth a day, couldn't get out of bed without a slug. This went on for over ten years. And every month I'd try to quit. Then, in October, 1967, we began a tour in Tulsa. When I met John there, I noticed something different.

"Carl," he said to me, "I haven't had a pill in two weeks. June had this fellow Dr. Nat Winston come out to see me. He really helped."

"John, that's great. You stick to your guns. You can lick it," I answered, smiling. But I wasn't so sure he would succeed after so many failures. He was hooked on amphetamines, sometimes as many as 25 a day. I have to admit I had mixed emotions. Part of me wanted him to win because I loved him; part of me wanted him to lose because if he did, then I could justify that my habit was unbeatable too. Day after day I watched him, but he kept winning, and now as I lay on the beach I wanted to win, too, more than anything. Perhaps with God on my side and the willingness to admit that without Him I could do nothing, I would make it.

And succeed Carl did, right up to the end. He died

a couple of years ago and he was a consistent witness for Christ. God kept him in the honky-tonks and his unique witness at the end of a show usually went something like this:

> Friends, now don't think I'm going to preach at you 'cause I'm not. I don't want you to feel guilty--feel happy. I'm working for the big man in the sky now and its the greatest thing that ever happened to me. You may not fully know why you're all here tonight, but I want to sing you a couple of songs that mean a lot to me. Clap your hands with me."

He would sing "Old Time Religion" and maybe two more old favorites, and the crowd usually joined in. Then he would say to them, "Can you imagine what it must sound like to God? Here you are in a nightclub singing to Him--now don't you ever quit."

Carl told me of an incident that really moved him.

> Usually when I finished the medley, the crowd would stand and clap. But there was one fellow I remember in particular who followed me out to the parking lot one night. "Are you gonna' do the same show tonight?" he asked.
>
> Not knowing what he had in mind, I answered timidly, "Well, yes, I thought we might." I waited and watched, and when he stuck out his hand I flinched a little inside. I could see something shiny in it.
>
> "I hadn't planned on coming back tonight, but if you're gonna' do the same show, I'll be here. I want you to have this--I was going to kill a man but I won't be needing it anymore." He handed me the most wicked-looking pig sticker in the world. Then for the first time, I noticed the tears. I encouraged him to follow the Lord. Later, I put the knife on my mantel at home as a reminder of someone who was helped because I

The Making Of A Prophet

had said a word for the Lord.

As fate would have it, I was almost finished writing Carl Perkins' life story when on August 16, 1977, Elvis Presley died of a heart attack in his Memphis mansion.

I called Carl down in Jackson and he was understandably stricken. He said to me:

> Val and I spent a real sad evening together last night because Elvis, though not a close friend of ours, did many things that indirectly aided my career. "Blue Suede Shoes" became a national hit because he had introduced it. He did more for country music than any man, with the possible exception of Hank Williams. They called him the "Hillbilly Cat" in the early days, and he rose from a $1.25-an-hour truck driver to a national legend before his 25th birthday. He really sang folk music for youth, just as Woody Guthrie sang for the dust bowl farmer. He fused black rhythm and blues with the rebelliousness of white youth and made "rock 'n roll" a household word. I just finished writing a farewell poem to him. I'll read it to you.
>
>> Elvis, I sat down to write about you,
>>> but it's tough to find a place to start.
>>
>> Through my mind runs many things,
>>> it lays heavy on my heart.
>>
>> I remember the early years--
>>> when our music was taking shape.
>>
>> Our visits to disc jockeys just to get it played.
>> And I remember people saying,
>>> "It's a fad, it's too wild, and it won't last too long,"
>>
>> But they didn't know you, Elvis,
>>> You were born to prove them wrong.

Ron Rendleman

I could see it in the early fifties,
    when our music was first played.
And I watched the magic of your magnetism
    as I stood there beside the stage,
Our music was well represented
    when you were on that stage,
And truly, history will record, my friend,
    that you did pave the way.
You opened many doors for a lot of us to go through.
    Thanks, my friend, you did it great--
    my song called "Blue Suede Shoes."

They call you "king," Elvis, but we both know
    there's only One.
And He called you home because His work for
    you on earth is done.
He always had, and always will have dominion
    and you know that's the reason why
He called you home for that great concert in
    the sky.
You'll always live among us, Elvis,
    there'll be no death to your songs.
Thanks again, you were my friend and I'll miss you--
    now that you're gone.

PS: Friend, there's one more thing I'd like to say.
A part of me and America died--when you passed away today.

One of the last things Carl said to me on the phone that day was:

The Making Of A Prophet

I'm going to miss old Elvis. For the last year or so I had a strong desire to see him. I felt a burden for him. I'd heard he'd become a recluse and wasn't taking care of himself. I wanted him to know he had a friend--a friend who had been to the bottom of life, who once had popularity and fame but who now is as content as he can possibly be. Sometimes now I lay in bed at night and think to myself, *Carl, why didn't you try to see him--God would have opened the door. You needed to let that old boy know you didn't need his money or his Cadillac gifts, but had just come to his house to eat corn bread and beans and a good strong onion and set and talk and say to him, "this ol' boy loves you."*

I don't think I'll miss many more opportunities to reach out to someone when I feel the Lord prompting me. I mean, those old friends need to know I love them, too, and that God can help them to a better life.

After Elvis was buried Carl said to me in another phone conversation:

> Ron, when someone who has touched your heart dies, it's always a sad time. But it hurts me to see how the world cries with the passing of a superstar like Elvis. When the true King came to earth to suffer those thorns and nails for man's redemption, only a few showed up at His funeral. And today, only a minority of the world's populace really honor Him and live according to His teachings.
>
> I've been doing a lot of watching and listening, and less talking, in the last few years and have learned an interesting thing or two about my fellow man. Regardless of where he's from, he suffers from what I like to call the superstar syndrome. Since he was created with a place inside him to be filled with the Spirit of God, but refuses to let God inhabit that place, he feels an awful emptiness and practices a form of idolatry--the

> worship of his fellow man. It seems to be more prevalent in modern times. Rudolph Valentino, James Dean, Elvis, or false Messiahs like Jim Jones or Sun Myung Moon are only a few examples. We will by nature follow someone, if not God, then a superstar or a world 'expert' who tells us how we should live, even what we should think.
>
> I have learned the hard way that Jesus Christ is the only Superstar worth following. He is the only expert who really has the answer to how we should live.

Of course I agree with Carl. And I might add, Presley reportedly had the same life changing experience at an early age that Cash and Perkins did. One could speculate that had he been as determined "to walk the line" as the other two finally did, he might still be alive today.

I next wrote *You Can't Fly Home Again*, a novel based on a true story about converted Dayak head hunters in Indonesia. That was done for Mission Aviation Fellowship and living with Dayaks in Indonesia for three weeks was one of the greatest experiences of my life.

Walking Into the Supernatural, Rudy Evensen's life story, was the next book I wrote. Interviewing colorful Rudy Evensen is an experience not easily forgotten. One particular story he told me because of its relevance to my own ministry will be ingrained in me forever. As Rudy related:

> When I was meeting with the "Men for Missions" I met a man who knew that I had been baptized in the Holy Spirit. He said his wife was demon possessed. His face was badly scratched so I asked him why.
>
> "She threw me through the screen door," he said.

The Making Of A Prophet

He was a big guy, about 250 pounds.

"Let's get in my car and go over to your house and I'll cast that demon out of her," I said, without hesitating. When we got to his house I started to follow him in but his wife, a nice looking petite woman about 40, blocked my way. "Where do you think you are going?" she asked.

"I'm going into the house."

"Over my dead body you are."

"Listen," I said, "the Bible says man is the head of the house and I have been invited here by your husband. I am coming in." I pushed her aside and went in. She ran into the kitchen where her husband was. Suddenly I heard a loud crash and I thought she must have thrown him through that screen door again. I stayed in the parlor, not knowing what to do. Then she came out of the kitchen, her eyes flaming, "Get out of here you blankety-blank," she yelled. But I didn't budge. "If you don't get out of here I'll call the police."

"You can call anybody you want," I said. She ran over to the phone and sure enough dialed the police. I just stood there, trying to figure out how to confront the demon I was sure she had. I witnessed to her for awhile, then finally, I just bowed my head and prayed, "Lord, when I lay my hands on her I want that demon to come out." I was praying with my eyes closed. The Bible says, "watch and pray." I understand now what that means because all of a sudden she struck me hard on the side of the face. It really hurt. I was about to defend myself when the doorbell rang. It was two policemen.

"What's the matter?" they asked.

"This man came in this house," she screamed, "he's an intruder!"

"Look, I'm a minister, I came here to pray for this

woman," I said.

"Is this right, lady?" one of them asked.

"He came with my no-good husband." One cop took her into the kitchen, to get us apart. The other stayed with me.

"What's going on here, Reverend?" he asked. "Why are you giving her a hard time?"

"A hard time? Look at the side of my face. She hauled off and whacked me one. She's got a demon. I came here to cast it out."

The other cop came out of the kitchen. "The Reverend here says that woman has a demon in her," the cop who'd been talking to me said. "He's going to cast it out."

"I believe she's got something," his partner said. "But you better get out of here, Reverend. You better not fool with her." I thought it over and, seeing that they weren't budging, decided to leave.

When I got into the car, I felt like bawling. My face was starting to swell up and my ear was ringing. "Jesus, what happened?" I cried out loud. "I just got the baptism. I have the power but the devil beat me up, Lord, and he used a woman on top of it. I don't go for men hitting women but I don't go for women hitting men, either."

All the Lord said was, *My son, I love you. But go where I send you.* I never forgot that lesson. Ever since I've tried only to go after praying and waiting for confirmation.

I lost track of Rudy Evensen long ago but those words, "go where I send you" have come back to me many times down through the years when I really needed to hear them for effective ministry.

My next three books, *Red Sky, A Line In The Sand,* and *Let The Games Begin* were novels that became a

The Making Of A Prophet

trilogy. They came about as a result of my listening to shortwave radio. (I'm a ham operator–K90EC.)

When I listened to the broadcasts of those who had been at the government sieges at Ruby Ridge, Idaho, and later at the Branch Davidian church at Waco, Texas, I knew we weren't getting the truth from mainstream media. I became alarmed that most Americans, and especially Christians, had no idea that America was rapidly deteriorating into a police state. My research confirmed to me that there are people in our government who are cooperating with globalists worldwide determined to bring America down, and force her to join a one-world *beast* government.

Most people have no idea how biased the mainstream media have become. Years ago they were respected and referred to as the "fourth estate" because they alone had the power to checkmate the three branches of government by keeping the public well informed. Today, news people are preoccupied it seems with being politically correct or in entertaining, rather than just reporting the facts. They remind me of puppets whose strings are being manipulated by a master puppeteer.

I self-published the last three books because they were too radical for *conservative* Christian publishers and *left-leaning* secular publishers, alike.

Red Sky, especially, seemed too unbelievable until the World Trade Center was destroyed. After that we could scarcely keep up with orders for the trilogy. Thinking people were asking questions.

Rejection in any form is always a bitter pill, but the rejection and ridicule I've received through the years have sometimes caused me to doubt my calling as a prophet. I remember taking *Red Sky* to three pastors in the small town I live near. I tried to go as a foot washer asking them to read the book and prepare their flocks for the great upheaval about to come. None were receptive and the Brethren pastor dropped dead a few months later quite unexpectedly. Coincidence?

But the Lord had the last word. He told me to go to all the churches in my area and put *Red Sky* on the car windshields while the members were attending Sunday service.

Prophets are generally accused of being alarmists, but history always confirms their message, if it is true. Scripture says God will always warn a society of His intentions through His prophets before He takes final action. Many of the things I've been saying and write about to warn family, and strangers alike, are now beginning to come to fruition. Though I haven't made a big income from my books through the years, many people have told me they've been helped by them.

When finances grew thin, I started **J.I.L.** (Jesus is Lord Limousine Co.) in South Elgin, Illinois. The devil tried to make me believe that potential customers would dislike the name, but I had a lot to be grateful for, and when I finally turned the business over to daughter, Rhonda, who had joined the company a few years earlier, we were running 15 cars and doing well in spite of the heavy-handed efforts of the government to over regulate.

After "Jesus is Lord" fellowship ended, I never found another group that I could call home. I visited many churches through the years, but always came away disappointed. Many of the "Jesus is Lord" people I run into from those precious years have told me the

The Making Of A Prophet

same sad story. We had experienced the wonderful presence of the Holy Spirit on a weekly basis--the healings, in fact, most of the manifestations of the Spirit the Bible relates, and we were spoiled for life. I know it's probably presumptuous to look back at a period of history when God worked in a unique way and want Him to work the same again, but I can't help it. I've tasted the best wine.

TOP: Interviewing Carl Perkins (at left) for the book *Disciple In Blue Suede Shoes*.
BOTTOM: Flying with MAF over Indonesia for the book *You Can't Fly Home Again*.

TOP: Ron plays the harmonica for Indonesian Bible students during a break from research on the MAF book.
BOTTOM: Meeting young Dayaks in the jungle on their way to market.

NINE

AT VARIOUS TIMES IN MY CHRISTIAN LIFE I have conversed with God. These are special times, and not very frequent, and usually come as a result of hungering and thirsting and great honesty. Some of us go for months, even years, without ever being totally honest with God. I have often told young people, "Whatever you do, don't play games with God. You can't fool Him so don't try. You don't feel like praying--tell Him, 'God, I really don't want to stay home tonight and pray and read my Bible--I'd rather be out with the crowd.'" You might be surprised to discover that He'll let you go for awhile, till one day you see how foolish the crowd's antics are, how little hope they have, and how the whole world trip is a poor substitution for a life with Him.

But in order to converse with God you must practice faith. Just like salvation, just like getting the baptism with the Holy Spirit, just like receiving a miracle, so it is with conversing with God. The first time it happened to me I had just read a fictional book by Serwood Wirt, entitled *Not Me, God,* in which a man has God speak to him while shaving one morning. A conversation between God and the man went on for months. That book got me thinking. Why, I asked myself, couldn't I have a conversation with God? Knowing what the scriptures say about God's desire to fellowship with His children, I was pretty sure I wouldn't upset Him too much by approaching Him this way.

At first, I'd ask a "yes" or "no" question. And I received answers that proved out in time. By faith, I had to believe that the very first answer I got was from God. The basis of my faith was His Word and that He always backs it up. I took James 1:5-6 and claimed it, "...if any of you lack wisdom let him ask of God who will give to all men liberally. But let him ask in faith, nothing wavering," etc.

That last part is very important, "nothing wavering." True faith must not waver. On one occasion, I couldn't believe the answer I received and decided I would ask God to repeat Himself. Seeing that the apostles had drawn lots to decide who would take Judas' place, I took out a coin and asked God to control the toss. You know the answer. I ended up going two out of three, then four out of seven. I was lost in confusion because I had let myself get double-minded. You see, faith says, "God, I accept the first answer, whatever it is. And I intend to act on it if it doesn't contradict scripture." God will honor your faith by answering, even if it's only to stop you.

Critics are quick to point out that this approach to God leaves one open to deceiving spirits. Yes, spirits will try to interfere. But I John 4:1 states: "Beloved, believe not every spirit but try (test) the spirits whether they are of God because many false prophets are gone out into the world. Hereby know ye the Spirit of God: every spirit that confesses Jesus Christ is come in the flesh is of God." So you ask the spirit, "Has Jesus Christ come in the flesh?" If a great peace settles over you, you're on the right track. Also, John 10:27 says, "My sheep hear my voice, and I know them and they follow me." Again, scripture must always support what you are hearing. That's another important reason why we need to know the Word of God.

After a season of this special communication with the Lord, He told me that in the future, He would mostly meet me in the Word. This was wise of Him because it re-emphasized the Word in my life. But remember, the last chapter is never written. That's what is so great about God. He is very creative and likes to do new and fresh things for us. But we prefer our religious ruts because they're so comfortable. You always know where the rut is going--because you've been down it so many times. You don't have to exercise faith at all.

The way I look at it, Christians should be the most creative people in the world. After all, they claim to follow the source of all creative energy--God, Himself. But go to their church services, notice how repetitious and easily forecasted they are. No wonder the world stays away.

I think this is why our Jesus rock concerts, or street meetings, or the chalk talks of Open Air Campaigners, or Mary Dominiques' ventriloquist dummy that touched the little ones at the county fairs were so effective--they're creative. But these are isolated exceptions and occur far too seldom in Christendom. Though I believe the King James Bible is the best version Christians can study, I take my hat off to Ken Taylor for his creative labor, the "Living Bible." Those who bum-rap it should go to the jails with us and listen to what the prisoners say about it--how much easier it is for them to read and understand. But you know, it takes a little to force yourself out of the rut sometimes. It takes courage to take that *first step*.

How can I forget one step of faith I took in the spring of 1971 when God told me to organize kids to hit a youth poverty march with tracts, and take our huge cross to a point where everyone of the 8,000 kids would have to pass. The devil kept telling me I would be sure to get arrested. But God had spoken. The place he led us to was in Wheaton, Illinois, about the half-way point of the 30-mile hike. The kids were strung out and walking in two's and three's and were bored to death. Many gladly accepted our material and in the weeks to follow the letters came in from those who had been provoked into thinking about God for the first time in their lives. I'll never forget how 90% of them would not look at our cross. I believe Romans 1 tells us why--because deep down, they know God exists, and the cross convicts them of their refusal to bend the knee to Him. We were asked several times not to pass out tracts, but I politely refused because of our Constitutional rights, and we were left alone.

There have been many such steps of faith that God has asked me to take. Another occurred in October of 1975. We were in Stockholm, rounding out a fruitful two-week evangelistic tour and were to have a youth rally in the largest church in Europe, the Filadelfia. The Lord told me in the morning that I would not be preaching in the evening service.

I stood before five hundred Swedish youth and through Henry Piirainen, our "far out" Swedish interpreter, told them that I didn't have the slightest idea what the meeting would be like but that I intended to turn it over to Jesus and wait on Him. I know many of them were caught short because they had come to be entertained by the American "Jesus People" in typical Pentecostal fashion. I guess I've been in too many such meetings. Let's face it, it's nice to have church entertainment that makes you feel good, but sadly, doesn't have the slightest effect on your life. It was impressed on me that the Lord wanted a "body" meeting where anybody who wants to is invited to get into the action as in I Corinthians 14:26.

As soon as I made my announcement and sat down the devil started his song and dance: *Now you've really blown it. They'll never invite you back because this is going to be a failure. No one will come up here from the audience, it's too much to expect from them.* The minutes passing seemed like endless hours. I kept praying, *Lord I'm trusting you totally.*

You talk about anxiety. I was fairly sure God would work, but how long would it take to penetrate fear and doubt in individuals' hearts in order for them to participate? I looked over at the youth pastor. He didn't seem too happy. I continued praying, and after what seemed forever, I heard footsteps. A long-haired Swedish youth using a crutch came up on the stage. You could have heard an angel sigh.

"I want to tell what the Lord has done for me," he began. "Four weeks ago I broke my leg. Some Christians prayed for me three days ago and the Lord healed me. I still use a crutch because my muscles are pretty weak. I'm pretty sure there are lots of us here who need a touch from the Lord. There are lots of people who need healing here tonight. God wants to fill people with His spirit. I never prayed for sick people before, but after my own healing, I have faith to do it. We prayed for a girl this morning and her leg grew out approximately an inch. But we people don't do anything, God does it. And to Him belongs all the glory."

Another boy spoke, then Mindy Lewis, the coed from Ohio who had traveled all the way to Sweden to attend school only to find Jesus three days earlier, gave a glowing testimony. Other testimonies came in rapid fashion, and then a song was offered by a girl who asked to use our guitar. The Holy Spirit was really moving now. Sven Lindahl, our elderly Swedish contact who had been responsible for working out our schedule, was weeping.

Just at this point the pastor jumped up and made an announcement that they would take an offering for the Americans. They called someone up to play the piano and a couple of their singers sang two songs, but you could actually feel the atmosphere of the place change. Dave, leader of the "Harvest," our music group, came over to my chair. "Hey, Ron, what goes? They just blew it."

"Yeah, I know," I answered, "but God is still around. And he's more powerful." After the offering I didn't get up, but just kept praying and the peace returned. Eventually, I closed the meeting by playing "He Touched Me" on the harmonica. As I look back now, I believe those young people were being shown how to really trust the Holy Spirit in a meeting and not man's traditions. But the devil was right about one thing-- before we even left the building, the word came to us that we would never be invited back. Oh well.

The Making Of A Prophet

I have met few Christians who are led by the Spirit of God one hundred percent of the time. I know I have missed the whisper of God many times only to be stopped abruptly by His shout. A shout can be another brother, the Bible, your family, or reproofs of society, like a traffic cop. These encounters usually are traumatic for us, but they are unnecessary if we would only turn up our hearing aid from the beginning.

Through much trial and error I began to understand what the real life of faith is--at least for me. I say it that way because I've gotten into many jams trying to tell God how I wanted to live by faith. Christian biographies of yesteryear are very inspiring, but they can also be a hang-up for a zealous Christian.

For instance, for a long time I really believed George Mueller's way (he once built orphanages in England) of *never* telling any human he had a need, but expecting God to supply, was the only way to live the faith life. So, for awhile, I never told anyone of my needs. One day when finances were down I said to God, "God, you always provide funds when we are in Your will. I know you don't want me back in a nine-to-five job, but I also know I haven't been going over to College of DuPage to talk with kids as often as I could, so, I promise you that I'll go every day from now on and I know you will take care of the food, and the rent, and my wife's confidence in me as a provider."

Three weeks of steady preaching later, I was in the worst hole ever and had to go out and make rounds on photographers for modeling work to pay the bills. I saw then that I mustn't look to anyone else's ministry, but God did have a blueprint I needed to follow each day to build my own house of faith with Him.

At first I would feel guilty not preaching everyday, but I began to realize God knew me better than I did. I grow weary of routine fairly quickly even when it's work directly related to the Kingdom. And God showed me that my day would never again be humdrum if I followed His blueprint and not mine.

Take hobbies for instance. Left to myself, I would run from project to project, devouring them, sacrificing family and friends in the process. So God let me do just that for awhile and I soon found that all the enjoyment in the hobby vanished because it had become a fixation rather than relaxation. Even after all these years of following God, I am amazed at how quickly earthly desires can invade my Christian life. The devil is expert at getting me to compromise and he does it in little increments so that I don't suspect anything and actively resist him.

The hardest and yet the most effective thing to do is resist the devil when any negative or anti-God thought enters my mind. "Resist the devil and he will flee from you." (James 4:7) Notice, there is no time element mentioned. He may not flee immediately, but he will flee. If God allows him to hang around occasionally, it's to teach us perseverance and to keep us from becoming a finger-snapping people.

Young people will often ask me, "How do you know the voice of the Lord, He never speaks to me?" Well He doesn't have to speak to be heard. The closer I am to Him, it isn't His voice I hear, but His mind that I *know*, His presence that I *feel*. I know what He wants me to do without a special delivery letter being sent down from heaven. Not that I have that special awareness constantly because I don't.

The Making Of A Prophet

Sometimes God has to practically use a club before I pay attention. One summer night I was praying out on my back porch under the stars when I received a thought out of context. It was, *don't leave A-Plus*. I kept on with my prayers, but the thought got stronger. You see, without asking God, I had decided to leave my modeling agency, A-Plus, where I had an exclusive agreement, because I felt they weren't getting me enough work. So I announced to them and all the other agencies that I would work on a nonexclusive basis. To ask A-Plus to take me back now was too much for my pride. I kept praying furiously, you know, like we do sometimes so we don't have to listen? But it was no use. After thirty minutes I finally said, "Okay, Lord, You win."

The next day I asked the agency to take me back and they were very receptive. Two weeks later they called me for a Nescafe TV commercial audition which I was not eager to do because I had had so many recent no win auditions. The casting gal at A-Plus must have called me back three times--something they never do. An agency doesn't beg their talent to accept work, they have too many eager actors to call on.

The audition went well. There must have been 20 guys waiting to read. It was what we used to call a "cattle call." I never liked to do a lot of lines on camera because I usually had trouble memorizing. But because of my writing background I could read a script well and almost fell over when the agency told me I won the commercial. There was only one catch. I would have a lot of lines, lines that I would somehow have to commit to memory.

"I can't do this," I said to myself and then I remembered to ask the Lord to help me out. I took a whack at the script and a week later showed up at the film studio feeling very nervous. The director shook my hand and announced, "Ron, we've changed your lines." Unbelievably, they had redone the entire commercial.

In the final rendition, I'm sitting on a couch holding a coffee cup. My Italian-looking wife walks over to me with a coffee pot and says, "Oh, I serve Nescafe all the time to the most particular coffee drinker in the world." I hold up my mug smiling a big toothy smile and say, "Fillerup." That's right, a long script had been cut to just one word. That night my prayers were full of praise.

Now for the punch line. That commercial ran for two years, netting me over thirty thousand dollars. I held the agency record for the most money made on one commercial for some time. The residual checks were never large enough to buy a new Corvette (God knew me too well), but every other Friday, it seemed, I'd get a call from the agency announcing they had a check for me for as much as fifteen hundred dollars. I knew everyone in that office was on a phone extension waiting for me to shout, "Praise the Lord."

I was still doing street work in those days and the money would always come in when our needs were the greatest. This was one of the many lessons in my life-long journey of learning to live by faith--that God is my provider, not the world system. But faith is always preceded by obedience. You can't have one without the other.

Just like that night in Sweden, the time I took 25 Jesus People with me. It was the last night of a hectic two weeks. The team had been without proper sleep or

The Making Of A Prophet

food and had traveled cramped in VW busses, and now sat around in a circle and took turns telling what the trip meant to them.

As I studied those young faces I realized how much I loved them. From the strong and sometimes overpowering personalities like "Sunshine" or Phil of "Morning Glory," (our music group) or tall Kent, to the quiet ones like Rick or Jeff, I saw how unique each was. Some had short hair, some long, some prayed and praised God vocally, others silently.

They all agreed the greatest single thing they had learned was how dear their flesh was to them. Most of them had never missed a meal in their lives, or a day without a bath, or had to share anything with anyone. To sneak out at night to find something to eat while team members did without was a great temptation which some succumbed to.

The Stockholm City Church had loaned us its coffee house for the evening and provided snacks. We started the meeting at eight and at midnight, had our first break. God began to squeeze my heart. He wanted me to wash their feet. I have washed the feet of young people before, but every situation is unique and this night, my first reaction was negative. It's always when we hesitate that turmoil and confusion and other forces come against us.

I finally prayed, *Okay God, you provide the pan for the water and the towel and I'll do the rest.* I dug around under the coffee bar and found a basin just right for the job. I filled it with lukewarm water and walked back into the center of the circle. A hush fell and people quietly resumed their seats without anyone saying a word. Up to this moment I thought the Lord wanted me to wash every member's feet. But the thought came to wash the feet of the strongest, proudest first, and three people came to mind--Craig, Kent, and "Sunshine." All three boys had ministries; all showed great potential as future leaders. I went to Craig first. He was the son of an eye surgeon in Wheaton and had been raised in the Wheaton Bible Church. He'd never seen a physical miracle till he had gotten involved in our ministry; our simplistic gospel seemed to be a healthy change of pace and a good balance to his Wheaton College training. I knelt before him and as soon as I touched his right foot, love for him filled my heart. Tenderly, I bathed his feet with my hands, caressing them as I felt Jesus must have done when He washed His disciples' feet. As I wiped his feet with the towel, I prayed for him and his ministry just loud enough so that only he could hear.

People were beginning to sob softly as the Holy Spirit began to fall. Suddenly, Craig was on his feet, face twisted in emotion, tears streaming. "I don't know about the rest of you," he cried, "but I'm giving notice right now that I'm serving God for the rest of my life. I'm following Him all the way, no matter the cost."

Next was Kent, and sure enough, as soon as his foot hit the water, I could hear him start to sniffle. Jesus was melting the pride and tempering the strong will that every leader has. He never takes it away but gives it an overhaul for greater endurance in hard times and increased sensitivity. A year or so later, Kent went into the army and after he successfully endured many testings and persecution, God used him in a tremendous way to touch the lives of many GIs.

"Sunshine" was the last. His given name was Gary

The Making Of A Prophet

Zeleski and when I first met him he had a hard time following his ego and Jesus too. He always got attention with his cut-up antics, and was soon to become one of the most effective teenage evangelists in the country. Born in California by parents that he seemed to lose contact with at a very early age, he became a doper but found Christ at 16. He was at the infamous Woodstock rock festival and was working in the drug rescue center where kids died in his arms from overdose. The futility of these deaths so unnerved him, he decided from then on never to be ashamed of Christ. Sadly, his 13-year-old brother tried one hit of LSD that had been cut heavily with strychnine (rat poison) and died.

Now as I began to wash his feet I wondered how he would react. Well, you would think he was being given a vision of heaven. He began to thank and praise Jesus and cry out in ecstasy. In reflection I feel it was partly because he had known so little affection in all his life. After I prayed for him the Lord told me to take my chair.

After several minutes of basking in the Lord's presence, I was distracted by someone moving around. The next thing I knew, someone was pulling off my boots and smelly socks. "Sunshine" was kneeling before me on the floor, with Becky Dohogne beside him, and they began to wash my feet. We were all crying now and even as I write this many years later, my eyes fill, just from remembering it. Becky was seventeen, came from a large family who had much strife, but she loved to sing for the Lord and any pride lurking in the corners of my heart that night got swept away by her drying my feet with her long auburn hair.

Ron Rendleman

Jesus, I pray for those kids at this moment. Thank you for using me to help them for a short period in their lives. Some of them have gotten away from you. But Lord, somehow get this book into their hands, and may each of them relive that precious night when You came down off your throne beside the Father and washed our feet. And Lord, may the Holy Spirit never let them forget, and me too, Lord, that the way we really minister for you on this earth is to be foot washers first, perhaps not always with water but by our attitudes, our actions and our love.

TEN

A HUNDRED AND TEN-STORY structure called the Sears Tower stands at Chicago's Franklin and Adams Streets. Supported by 76,000 tons of steel, this "Gargantua" houses 16,500 workers and cost $150 million dollars to erect!

I stood at noon hour on a sunny day looking up at the towering monument being erected, and was amazed at man's ingenuity. At the same time I was sickened by stupidity in wasting so much effort and money while people living in ghettos within a block of the building had little to eat. I recalled an incident in the Old Testament when another tower was built.

At that time all mankind spoke a single language. As the population grew and spread eastward, a plain was discovered in the land of Babylon and was soon thickly populated. The people who lived there began to talk about building a great city, with a temple tower reaching to the skies--a proud, eternal monument to themselves.

The Bible goes on to say how God intervened and caused confusion and the workers couldn't understand each other. They spoke different languages, and to this day, their descendants can't communicate without interpreters--and just like the rainbow, remains a testimony to the time when man placed himself above God. After the great flood caused by the wickedness of man, God told Noah he would place a rainbow in the sky as a testimony to man that He would never again destroy the earth with a flood. (Genesis 9:12-17)

The Sears Tower is symbolic of man's insane drive to achieve, to fill the great vacuum within because he is so God-barren. A colossal steel-concrete tombstone, a pagan sacrificial altar, stained with at least seven workmen's lives, barren of any lasting contribution, or any consequence, just there.

This day the sidewalks were packed with people on their lunch break, secretaries in their tight sweaters and short skirts hurried by and I must admit I spent more time than I ought watching God's creation. That night as I knelt to pray, God nailed me immediately with lust.

"But Lord," I argued, "I didn't take them to bed in my mind as I once might have."

Your problem was lust of the eye, He told me. I was reminded of I John 2:15: "Love not the world, neither the things that are in the world. If any man love the world, the love of the Father is not in him. For all that is in the world, the lust of the flesh, and the lust of the eye, and the pride of life, is not of the Father, but is of the world."

"But Lord, I still don't understand," I pled.

He answered: *Anything that captivates your attention to the point of feeding your carnal nature, but not your spirit is wrong. It is true that beauty was created but the creature cannot replace the Creator. Even to sit in an art museum all day and gaze at great works of art*

The Making Of A Prophet

is wrong if it replaces priorities.

"Father, I get the point and I confess that you are right. I'm still in bondage to a pretty face or figure. But You said I could become free, now tell me how."

All lust is fathered by selfishness. When your gaze lingers on a pretty girl you are satisfying your soul--it is a selfish act, you are coveting. In the future, when you look at a girl, see her from My point of view. Turn your lust into My love. Immediately say to your soul, "Jesus loves her. He died for her. He can give her all the love she so desperately searches for by seeking the attention of men by her mannerisms and attire."

The next day when the wind caught a skirt the Lord reminded me of our conversation, and without hesitating, I simply thought, *Jesus loves her so much, if she only knew.* Magically, something beautiful began to happen. I sensed a freedom, a fatherly love and a closeness of the Lord simultaneously. For a long time after, I stayed out of bondage to lust. But if I forgot the principle, back into bondage I would go--and bondage is the most frustrating thing for a Christian to experience after he has tasted freedom.

I mention this as background for what happened next. Business took me near the Sears Tower around noon quite regularly while it was under construction. I had seen the workmen sitting on the sidewalk having their sandwiches, almost two hundred of them, lined up with their backs against the buildings or sitting on the curb, and I never thought much about it till the Lord opened my eyes one day. To liven up their lunch break they had come to gawk at the young girls passing by. As I watched, the next girl turned the heads of every man, progressively, like a wave of the sea, as she passed.

And then I saw something else. Some of the men had gotten down low on the sidewalk so that they could see under the skirts. A burden came over me. But lest I became their judge, I was reminded that at one time in my life I was quite capable of the same grossness, and then some. Still, I was bothered.

A day or two later on my way to Chicago I got an idea. I stopped at a religious bookstore and purchased two hundred tracts by the Chick organization entitled *This Was Your Life*, a little booklet that graphically shows a man dying and being ushered into heaven where he finds himself watching details of his sordid life on a panoramic movie screen. It was perfect for the workers.

The next day I parked my Pontiac on a side street and waited. When the men came out as usual at noon, I started down the long line of yellow helmets and about all of the men accepted the tracts. A few made wisecracks but I didn't stop. When I finished with Franklin Street I walked along Adams and when I got to the last man, unbelievably, I had one tract left. I gave it to a gal at a bus stop. I praised the Lord right there and then started back up the line. A couple of young guys were really ridiculing the booklet so, smiling, I squatted down in front of them.

"You know," I began, "I gave you that because I've found the answer to life and I want other guys to find it too--and it's not in sex, booze or making fifty thousand a year."

"Yeah, well you got your thing, I got mine," this young good-looking Italian lays on me, all the time trying to see a girl passing behind me. This brought

The Making Of A Prophet

smirks from the men sitting on either side.

"*Playboy* used to be my Bible," I continued, "but I have found something much better. I mean, sin is fun, I won't deny that--but it doesn't satisfy, not really. The more you get, the more you want. And always, there's that vague emptiness deep inside that sex, booze, or a solid gold Cadillac can't satisfy." I paused to let that sink in and looked directly into his eyes. His smirk slowly faded, and then in those handsome eyes, I saw Satan. The man got up quickly with his friends and left.

I bowed my head right there and prayed for them. According to Jesus' own words, most people are not going to heaven because, "the highway to hell is broad, and its gate is wide enough for all the multitudes who choose its easy way. But the gateway to life is small, and the road is narrow, and only a few ever find it." (Matthew 7:14)

I looked up toward the sky, to where I would someday meet Jesus, but there was little sky--just that colossal tower of Babel, grotesquely defiant. The workmen were all gone now, drawn back to the mother-monster who would continue to feed and clothe them and give them all the "good things" of life.

ELEVEN

TOO MANY CHRISTIANS have elevated their family doctors to the right hand of the Father. The way I read my Bible, a doctor should be called only *after* a long-distance call, person-to-person, is made to the master physician Himself--Jesus. The conversation might go something like this:

"Jesus, I have to talk to you."

"I know, I've been waiting."

"Yes, well you see, this is so difficult to talk to you about, it's so new to me, but I'm really at my wits' end. Little Johnny has those pains in his chest again."

"The evil one is afflicting him."

"Yes, well...uh, I wouldn't know about that, but what should I do? I gave him the medicine the doctor prescribed but it hasn't been helping at all."

"I know, it is not anointed."

"What does that mean?"

"I have lifted my hand from it."

"Why?"

"Because I have a new thing to show you."

"What do you mean?"

"You have replaced prayer with medicine."

"Oh."

"You have made your doctor a god."

"But my pastor, in fact, everyone I know says that You can work through doctors."

"I can and I do, but I don't need them to heal. Nor do I desire that my children bend the knee to man."

"Have I done that?"

"When the boy was first attacked what was your reaction?"

"I....I....telephoned the doctor. Oh, I see, I forgot all about you."

"Yes, you did. But now turn to James 5:14-16 of my Word."

"All right, I have found it. It says, 'Is any sick among you? Let him call for the elders of the church; and let them pray over him, anointing him with oil in the name of the Lord; and the prayer of the faith shall save the sick, and the Lord shall raise him up; and if he has committed sins, they shall be forgiven him. Confess your faults one to another, and pray one for another, that you may be healed. The effectual fervent prayer of a righteous man availeth much.' Wow! How long has that been in the Bible, I never saw it before?"

"Almost two-thousand years."

"But why doesn't my pastor ever mention it on Sunday morning?"

"Because Sunday morning is very important to him. He and his followers draw nigh unto me with their mouths and honor me with their lips but their hearts are far from me; in vain they do worship me, teaching for doctrines the commandments of men."

"Oh, Jesus, these are hard words to hear. I am one of his followers and I took everything he said to be the truth."

The Making Of A Prophet

"You did not search my Word, rightly dividing the Word of truth."

"Lord, I see my error, please forgive my laziness and my lack of belief in your Word. Just tell me what to do and I'll do it."

"Pray for the pastor. Then go to him and entreat him, properly as an elder, with these scriptures. Ask him to come and pray when there is sickness in your house, confessing your faults. Do not leave the church until I tell you to do so. But continue to pray for it."

"Lord, I will do it. Is there anything else?"

"Yes, keep hungering and thirsting for me."

"Thank you, Lord, I'll try. Oh, yes, what do I do about the doctor?"

"Witness to him, he needs to be saved. Go now to Johnny. Your obedience has made him whole."

I realize I may have stretched your imagination some but I trust you get the point. The doctor has his place and it's not at the right hand of the Father. I, and members of my family, do see a doctor occasionally. My daughter was treated by a dermatologist for acne and I had an annoying wart burned off by a doctor. My wife and I go to the dentist and visit a chiropractor. There's freedom to do this once you know the mind of God in the matter.

But many, if not most, Christians really don't fervently seek God when they become sick--they run for the phone to make a doctor appointment, little realizing that they are putting the world system before the Father. And we know from scripture who controls that. Remember, in Matthew 4:8-9? "Again the devil took Him (Jesus) up into an exceeding high mountain and showed Him all the kingdoms of the world and the glory of them and said to Him, *all these things will I give thee* if you will fall down and worship me." Obviously, the devil could not give away something he did not totally control.

Perhaps, at an early time in America's history most doctors were righteous men who used prayer and God's intended natural methods to help healing--like fasting, herbs, poultices and silver water. But just as prophesied, men's hearts grew ever increasingly lustful for personal gain and the medical practice in the past 50 years in America has been on a downward spiral.

The process was accelerated with the discovery of penicillin by Dr. Alexander Fleming. Chemists were stymied because they couldn't grow mold fast enough to make this antibiotic commercially viable. During World War II, they discovered a way to make it synthetically and a new era was born in medicine. It became the rage among doctors, much to the delight of the drug companies. Very soon patented synthetic chemicals began making drug companies very wealthy.

A book, *Amazing Medicines the Drug Companies Don't Want You to Discover*, states that these companies won't sell a medicine they can't patent. So *goodbye* natural healing remedies, and *hello* to a stream of pharmaceuticals.

But from the beginning, the supposedly wonderful penicillin had problems. Many people were allergic to it and suffered from shock, rashes, hives and some died. That's why doctors still ask, "Are you allergic to penicillin?" Since the 1940s, chemists have created numerous penicillin-type antibiotics to avoid allergy problems and because each type only killed certain organisms. In other words, you can't use the same anti-

The Making Of A Prophet

biotic to kill a throat infection on someone who has a skin infection.

Medical scientists say that some doctors hand out antibiotics like candy regardless of whether they will help the person or not. Some prescribe them for preventing colds, but *antibiotics absolutely will not prevent a cold*. "Approximately one-fifth of the antibiotic prescriptions are unnecessary or won't work," says Dr. Steve Waterman, chief of epidemiology at the California Department of Human Services. "It's sloppy medical practice, but it's very common."

Medical information in the US is now almost 100 percent drug company controlled. With the advent of synthetic drugs, these companies offered medical schools grants and other perks if they would teach their students about the latest designer drugs. Today, practically all medical research done in the US is drug company financed. Furthermore, these companies send out highly paid sales reps who shower doctors with gifts. Gone are the days when doctors just received free samples and note pads. Today they're treated to sumptuous dinners, computers, free vacations and generous grants, all to the tune of over $165 million a year, or approximately $13,000 per MD who only gets, at most, one hour of nutrition training in the eleven years he spends in medical school.

Cancer treatment is second only to oil as a money maker worldwide. Little wonder any "cures" other than AMA endorsed are labeled quackery and their promoters mercilessly persecuted. A report published in *Current Cancer Research* states that only seven percent of the people treated with chemotherapy showed any remission.

Ron Rendleman

The FDA, the watchdog of the industry, is a player in this conspiracy and approves dozens of dangerous drugs every year despite negative test results. The General Accounting Office reported that over an eight-year period, about 50 percent of all FDA approved drugs had serious risks such as heart failure, convulsions, birth defects, and blindness. In fact, side effects from drugs put a million-and-a-half people in the hospital every year and about 160,000 of those people die.

It seems that ambitious young ladder climbers know that the best way to get high-paying drug company jobs is to put their time in working for the FDA, and they're not about to bite the hand that will someday feed them.

In 1969, the Surgeon General of the United States declared, "We can close the book on infectious diseases caused by bacteria." Little did he know that those bacteria were apparently smarter than the chemists who created the antibiotics and have developed an immunity through normal evolutionary processes.

The occurrence of infectious diseases is rising dramatically--not just in third world countries, but also here in the US. Scientists are getting very worried that we won't find new chemicals to fight them. For example, there are several tuberculosis strains that are resistant to all antibiotics and last year in Cincinnati, there was an 838 percent increase (over the yearly average) in whooping cough among children who *had been vaccinated*.

Everyday, new evidence surfaces that reveals vaccinations of all types have been compromised with pollutants such as formaldehyde, aluminum, mercury, (used as stabilizers) and under the guise of waging war

The Making Of A Prophet

on terrorism, the government is now proposing compulsory smallpox and even anthrax inoculations. **Not in my household!** The truth about vaccines is slowly emerging:

> Members of the Association of American Physicians and Surgeons (AAPS) passed a resolution at their 57th Annual Meeting in St. Louis, calling for an end to government-mandated childhood vaccinations. It was passed without a single "no" vote.
>
> "Our children face the possibility of death or serious long-term adverse effects from mandated vaccines that aren't necessary or that have very limited benefits," said Jane M. Orient, MD, the Executive Director of AAPS.
>
> "This is not a vote against vaccines," said Dr. Orient. "This resolution only attempts to halt blanket vaccine mandates by government agencies and school districts that give no consideration for the rights of the parents or the individual medical condition of the child. Forty-two states have mandatory vaccine policies, and many children are required to have 22 shots before first grade. On top of that, as a condition for school attendance, many school districts require vaccination for diseases such as hepatitis B, primarily an adult disease, yet children under 14 are three times more likely to suffer adverse effects (including death) following the hepatitis B vaccine than to catch the disease itself."
>
> In late October, students in Utica, N.Y. were sent home from school and told they could not return until they'd received hepatitis B vaccinations. Further, parents were threatened by Child Protective Services with possible seizure of their children, based on "education neglect."
>
> "It's obscene to threaten to seize a child just because his parents refuse medical treatment that is ob-

viously unnecessary and perhaps even dangerous," said Dr. Orient. "AAPS believes that parents, with the advice of their doctors, should make decisions about their children's medical care--not government bureaucrats. This resolution affirms that position."

Source: www.healthmall.com/newsletter.cfm, November 2, 2000.

Doctor Len Horowitz of Idaho who wrote the well documented books, *Death in the Air* and *Emerging Viruses* charges that certain members of the Rockefeller-driven industrial-pharmaceutical industry created the AIDS virus, loosed it on unsuspecting Africans and homosexuals in America, then made millions on drugs to supposedly help fight the disease. He claims that Ebola, Hepatitis and the most recent scare, West Nile Virus, were all developed in American company pharmaceutical labs.

That this agenda dovetails nicely with Rockefeller-sponsored CFR's published goals of reducing the world's population by at least one half, should come as no surprise to anyone who has researched the diabolical plans of the "one worlders." Skeptics are urged to do further research.*

One day the Lord showed me that He is more glorified when His people live healthy lives by obeying His health laws and the Holy Spirit's promptings than He is when they go forward for healing every time a "healing" evangelist comes to town. And I realized, sadly, that here was still another area where the church has missed God.

*Doctor Horowitz's website is: Healing celebrations.Com. His phone number is 888-508-4787.

The Making Of A Prophet

God's dietary laws given in Leviticus II and Deuteronomy 14 show us which foods are unhealthy, in fact, every unclean animal or bird listed is a scavenger. A hog will eat every putrid thing he finds, has but one poorly constructed stomach and very limited excretory organs. In about four hours after he has eaten offensive matter, man may eat the same secondhand off the hog's ribs. According to Elmer A. Josephson, health researcher, "It was reported recently from a lab of one of our northern universities that trichina (trichinosis) laden swine flesh was heated to 600 degrees Fahrenheit and then put under a microscope. To the amazement of the technicians, some worms were still alive and moving about." Senator Thomas C. Desmond, who served as chairman of the New York Trichinosis Commission stated, "Physicians have confused trichinosis with some fifty ailments, ranging from typhoid fever to acute alcoholism."

If we ignore God's Word, and the leading of the Holy Spirit by eating to please our tastes, or pushing ourselves beyond reason in work, sex, or pleasure, we will reap what we sow. The overweight pastor who dropped dead at forty-two climbing stairs did not have his "number come up." He was reaping what he sowed. God says, "Know ye not that ye are the temple of God, and that the Spirit of God dwelleth in you? If any man defile the temple of God, him shall God destroy..." Corinthians 3:16-17. Christians love to quote these verses to alcohol or tobacco users, but rarely see the application to their own sin of gluttony.

From past experiences of unsuccessfully getting people to change their eating habits, I've come to really see the various ways Satan has control of God's children. I was convicted by the Holy Spirit for a year about drinking coffee and its harmful effects on the body though I was only having a cup a day. It took me that long to quit. For me, even one cup was too much because it would make me tense and affect how I dealt with others. Satan, the Bible says, is prince of the air. He's also prince of the airwaves. Invariably, most foods heavily advertised on television are not only lacking in nutrition, but are downright harmful. For every TV commercial selling fresh fruit or vegetables, there are a hundred selling TV dinners, pizza, coffee, soft drinks, or fruit drinks (colored water).

The first step back to walking on the King's highway toward better health is to admit to God that you have abused His temple and that Satan has been controlling your eating habits. To help break his power, start fasting. I'm always amazed at how seldom this is addressed by pastors from the pulpit--another sad indictment. One secret of the power of the early Methodists was their fasting and praying. John Wesley, in a sermon on fasting in 1789 said, "While we were at Oxford, the rule of every Methodist was to fast every Wednesday and Friday in imitation of the primitive church."

"This practice of the early church was universally allowed. 'Who does not know,' says Epiphanius, an ancient church writer, 'that the fast of the fourth and sixth days of the week--Wednesday and Friday--are observed by Christians throughout the world?'"

Satan hates fasting and will try to break down your will by exaggerating hunger pangs, weakness and even sick feelings, but don't give in for blessings will follow! Regular fasting forces the body to burn fatty deposits and other impurities in the blood, detoxifying the body. It gives the heart and other vital organs a much needed rest. Fasting can actually save your life. The Chinese have used it to cure disease for centuries. The principle is that, given half a chance, the body will mend itself. Liquid, either water or raw fruit juices, (not canned, or even frozen) should be taken every two hours to help flush out the poisons. Start slowly, skipping one or two meals, until you can go the whole day. My daughter, Vicki, once fasted for 23 days when she was 17, without ill effects. Come off the fast gradually too. Don't gorge yourself, for you'll undo all the good.

As for diet, try and get back to the natural as much as possible. Why eat canned beans when green beans in a salad are not only more delicious but 100 times more nutritious? Why eat canned applesauce when an apple is available? Remember, any time you heat food over 110 degrees you destroy the life-giving enzymes. You may maintain life with dead food, but you won't have the vitality and disease-fighting capability that only live food can give.

Common sense care of one's body honors God. There is no need for fanaticism in selecting or preparing foods or jogging fifty miles a week. But God gives us two ends: one to think with, the other to sit on. Our future depends on which end we use. Heads we win; tails we lose.

TWELVE

NON-SCRIPTURAL PRACTICES of born-again believers in recent years have increased dramatically. I've already touched on the gifts of the Spirit, living by faith, education, dispensationalism, eating habits, etc. Now, I must add still another practice that dishonors God--birth control.

Today's Christian woman, because of lack of proper church teaching, has turned to the world's experts who gladly tell her how to live, how to think, how to raise her children, or how to avoid having them. The following reasons are those most often used by ministers, marriage counselors, doctors, and other present day "experts" to help women justify using birth control devices or even have abortions.

1. A woman is capable of directing her own life. She has the freedom to use God's gifts according to her own.

2. Woman was not created primarily for the propagation of the species, but "because it was not good for man to be alone." (Genesis 2:18)

3. Nothing is more detrimental to a child than to feel unwanted.

4. Mother's health.

5. The physical, emotional, spiritual, economic, and educational needs of all the children in the family cannot be met.

6. Genetically transmitted illness.

7. Over-population, an estimated six-and-one-half billion on earth.

8. The couple just doesn't like children.

While from a humanist viewpoint, any one of these reasons might appear to justify practicing birth control, the seeking Christian woman is wise to turn to the Bible as her final word. While the New Testament has no direct mention of birth control, the New and Old have as their focal point that life is precious to God and He wishes us "to be fruitful and multiply." (Genesis 1:22) Incredibly, He has gone into partnership with mankind allowing us to participate as co-authors in creation. It is even more incredible that mankind would usurp His authority and hinder that creative process.

Notice, practically every reason listed above has self interest, fear, or lack of faith in God as its root. Even "mother's health" places the mother's welfare over God's possible plan to bring a baby into the world for His particular purposes. Too few Christians realize that controlling birth is an act of ungratefulness toward God since scripture points out that children are His gifts to man. "Lo, children are a heritage of the Lord: and the fruit of the womb is His reward." (Psalm 127:3) And, "Happy is the man that his quiver is full of them (children): they shall not be ashamed but they shall speak with the enemies in the gate." (Psalm 127:5)

The argument that we must control over population does not establish the morality of birth control any more than war does. Nor are social problems the result of high fertility. They are the result of the depraved nature of man. "Genetically transmitted illness" is perhaps the strongest argument listed, but it implies that God makes mistakes. Exodus 4:11 states, "...and the Lord said unto him (Moses), who hath made man's mouth? Or who maketh the *dumb* or *deaf*, or the *seeing*, or the *blind*? Have not I, the Lord?"

C. Everett Koop, MD, retired Surgeon General stated in his book, *The Right to Live, the Right to Die*: "The following letter to the editor appeared in the *Daily Telegraph* in London on December 8, 1962, when the Thalidomide tragedy was being discussed in European newspapers and abortion was sought as an easy way to get rid of the possibly defective babies:

> Sirs: We were disabled from causes other than Thalidomide, the first of us having two useless arms and hands; the second, two useless legs; the third, the use of neither arms nor legs.
>
> We were fortunate...in having been allowed to live and we want to say with strong conviction how thankful we are that none took it upon themselves to destroy us as useless cripples.
>
> Here at the Delarue School of Spastics, one of the schools of the National Spastic Society, we have found worthwhile and happy lives and we face our future with confidence. Despite our disability life still has much to offer and we are more than anxious, if only metaphorically, to reach out toward the future.
>
> This, we hope, will give comfort and hope to the parents of the Thalidomide babies, and at the same time serve to condemn those who would contemplate the destruction of even a limbless baby.
>
> Yours faithfully,
> Elane Ducket, Glynn Verdon, and Caryl Hodges

Dr. Koop practiced medicine as a pediatric surgeon. He specialized in correcting birth deformities of every nature: twisted legs, cleft spines, bladders inside out, etc. He wrote, "I treated a boy who had 25 operations. I see him and his family in the community about once a week. They are a great family and consider the boy and his problems to be the best experience life has offered them. The boy is a delight. He has strengthened the family and has taught them compassion and understanding."

A personal note--when my wife became pregnant with our fifth child, Roy, about the third month she unknowingly had coffee with a neighbor who had the measles. The doctors told us the baby could be retarded or deformed. Legally, she could have had an abortion. Though I wasn't a Christian, I felt, and she agreed, that she should have the child. The doctors were right but through the years we have come to believe he is a special gift from God. Now he is a delight on those otherwise lonely nights, since all the other kids have left home. God has taught us patience and many other dear lessons through him.

There has been much "wildfire" about the side effects of oral contraceptives, a lot of which is unsubstantiated. But though many women say they experience little, if any effects, research shows definite shortages of vitamin B and other vitamins in users of the "pill." There have also been substantial evidences of thrombosis (blood clotting), loss of hair, nausea, headaches, break-through bleeding, liver damage, increase in breast size, breast milk stoppage, and a few others. Again, effects vary greatly in each user, but the unavoidable question is, can such interference to nat-

The Making Of A Prophet

ural body chemistry be pleasing to God?

It seems incredible that Christian women will admit to using birth control methods, but have never done scripture study to affirm their action. There may be some, who after studying simply don't see it, or will admit their faith is weak, or feel they should continue the practice for other reasons. Regardless, I still believe they'll be operating in God's Plan B, His second best plan for their lives.

But for those who are seeking a better way, consider the following. God, in His great wisdom, has a birth control plan which does work for those who are operating by faith and totally submissive to His Holy Spirit. The natural law of fecundity in itself causes a separation in the succession of births a woman may have. She cannot become pregnant every time the seed is planted. In fact, she can only conceive for one week during her entire monthly menstrual cycle. Even then, one-third of all fertilized eggs will abort naturally. A Spirit-filled marriage should have a natural timing and rhythm in harmony with God's natural laws of fecundity so that His perfect will can be carried out. Such a marriage will not have excess, and there will be abstinence from time to time, as Paul mentions in I Corinthians 7:5.

As one young married brother so pointedly put it: "Married Christians need to know the difference between love and lust. Love always wants to give, lust can't wait to get. Many Christians lust after their wives and call it love. Some are even blissfully committing legalized rape. Taking the pill definitely promotes irresponsibility and excess--a kind of license to lust, especially with unmarried women."

The Old Testament is rich with faith-building examples of God's ability to create or stop life in the womb. He was able to open Leah's, Rachael's, and Sarah's wombs, and of course, Mary's, mother of Christ. He was able to shut the womb of Hannah and the whole household of Abimelech. (Genesis 20:18)

Well over a hundred thousand people in America are sterilized each year, but this practice was forbidden in the Old Testament. "There shall not be a barren male or female among you." Coitus interruptus was not tolerated either. (Genesis 38:9-10) Artificial insemination would be unacceptable for the same reason, in that it involves spilled seed and an unholy trinity that could be derived from Matthew 19:5, "...for this cause shall a man leave father and mother, and shall cleave to his wife: and they twain shall be one flesh."

God's Word states, "Be anxious for nothing; but in everything by prayer and supplication with thanksgiving let your requests be made known unto God." (Philippians 4:6) And, "He that doubteth is damned if he eat, because he eats not of faith: for whatsoever is not of faith is sin." (Romans 14:23) "The just shall live by his faith." (Habakkuk 2:4)

While it is quite normal for a woman to have difficulty putting faith in God in as personal an issue as this, the spiritual part of her cries out for the will of the Father. In this attitude, the spiritual woman might say to the Father, "Father, I commit my husband, my right to have a particular number of children, and especially our time of lovemaking to you. I'm not dumb enough to expect you to close my womb as a safeguard to our excess, but I am asking you to align our desires for each other with your highest will for us.

The Making Of A Prophet

We offer ourselves as living sacrifices for your purposes which is our reasonable service. Therefore, we are going to praise you for each and every child, believing that these are your gifts and that you will make a way to provide for them."

Finally, I leave you with a thought that's not carelessly conjured to tickle ears but to give credence to concept.

The year is around 13 AD. The apostle, Peter, who has been out preaching the gospel for a couple of months, is home for the weekend. Having shipped the kids off to the mother-in-law, he and his woman have a long overdue weekend alone together all planned at a resort by the Sea of Galilee. It's a bright sunshiny day as they pack their donkey and begin the journey. But before they've gone a hundred meters, the Mrs. stops, gasps, and runs back to their humble dwelling. She returns soon, out of breath.

"What did you forget, dear?" asks Peter.

"The pills."

"Pills?" asks Peter.

"You know, dear, the pills I'm supposed to take every morning so that I don't get..."

"Oh, yes," interrupts the great man of faith, sighing gratefully. "It's good you remembered. Now we can relax and be free from worry. The way our economy is going, that's all I need--another mouth to feed."

And the two take each other's hand and continue down the dusty road.

THIRTEEN

AS I RE-READ THAT LAST CHAPTER I've got to believe very few Christians will probably agree with it, or for that matter, many concepts in this book. I don't have a lot to say in defense. Some have tried to "straighten me out" but I'm not marching to their beat. I don't claim to have all the answers--but what little knowledge I have gained with God's help, I've tried to faithfully pass on to others. Since you're still hanging around, I'd like you to consider a few more examples of Christian practices and beliefs that are totally unscriptural.

For instance, Christ died on a Friday, right? Wrong! The truth is that Christ died on a Wednesday. Eleven different times our Lord said that He would remain in the grave three days and three nights. He said that, just as Jonah was three days and three nights in the belly of the fish, He would spend three days and three nights in the heart of the earth. (Matthew 12:40)

If Jesus was crucified on Friday afternoon and was raised on Sunday morning, as is commonly believed and taught, then His Word failed. He said that He would be in the grave three days and three nights, and you can't figure more than two nights from Friday afternoon to Sunday morning, to save your life.

But you might ask, "What difference does it make what day our Lord was crucified?" It makes all the difference in the world. It is necessary that we believe the Bible if we are Christians. We may not understand it all, but God expects us to believe it all because it is His Word.

Another false teaching is that Christ supposedly arose on Sunday morning. The truth of the matter is that our Lord arose from the dead late on Saturday afternoon. "In the end of the Sabbath, as it began to dawn *toward* the first day of the week, came Mary Magdalene and the other Mary to see the sepulcher. And behold, there was a great earthquake: for the angel of the Lord descended from heaven, and came and rolled back the stone from the door, and sat upon it...And the angel...said unto the women...I know that ye seek Jesus, who was crucified. He is *not* here: for He is *risen*..." (Matthew 28:1-6)

Notice, the tomb was *already empty* when the women came to it. Second, the women visited the tomb very late on Saturday just as Sunday was beginning. Remember that the Jewish day always began at sundown, while our day begins at midnight. In Leviticus 23:32 the Lord said, "From even unto even shall ye celebrate your Sabbath." So the evidence is clear: when the women came to the sepulcher, it was not on Sunday, the first day of the week, but late on Saturday afternoon. Notice the scripture says: "In the end of the Sabbath (Saturday), as it began to dawn (draw on) toward the first day of the week (Sunday), came Mary Magdalene and the other Mary to see the sepulcher." (Matthew 28:1)

The Making Of A Prophet

Still another false teaching is the celebration of Easter. It is not in the Bible. The word "Easter" occurs only one time in Acts 12:4, and even there the correct translation of the word should be "Passover." Check the Greek if you don't believe it.

If God had intended for us to celebrate the resurrection of Christ, He would have put it in His Word. God tells us in His Word how we are supposed to worship, how we are supposed to give money for His cause, how we are to celebrate the Lord's Supper; but when it comes to observing Easter, you won't find one hint of it.

Webster's New International Dictionary, first edition, states that the name "Easter" comes from the Anglo-Saxon "Eastre," the name of "a goddess of light or spring, in honor of whom a festival was celebrated in April." Easter can be traced back to the days of the Phoenicians, Babylonians, and Chaldeans, who lived thousands of years before Christ. These pagan nations kept a spring festival in honor of the goddess Astarte, or Ishtar, who, as a goddess of spring, had rabbits that laid eggs. The eggs symbolized a new life and the colored eggs signified a wish for a bright new year ahead. Both the rabbit and the egg are pagan symbols of sex and fertility.

What about Easter sunrise services? The Bible says it is the most abominable kind of idolatry: "Turn thee yet again and thou shalt see greater abominations than these. And He brought me into the inner court of the Lord's house and behold, at the door of the temple of the Lord between the porch and the altar, were about five and twenty men with their backs to the temple of the Lord and their faces toward the east; and they worshipped the sun toward the east...and though they cry in mine ears with a loud voice, yet will I not hear them." (Ezekiel 8:15-18)

Here God is condemning Israel for taking part in sunrise services, and yet multiplied thousands of people will get up early on Easter morning to watch the sun come up over the horizon thinking they are celebrating the resurrection of Christ. God calls this the most abominable of all worship.

And what about Christmas, still another perversion of truth? During the first three centuries, Christians did not celebrate birthdays, even Christ's. Paul and the other epistle writers made it clear not to observe days, years, etc. Actually, observing birthdays was another pagan custom and Christians apparently believed that if you didn't know God, then you had little else to live for except yourself, so observing your birthday became very important.

Paul wrote in Galatians 4:9-10 "But now, after that ye have known God, or rather are known of God, how turn ye again to the weak and beggarly elements, whereunto ye desire again to be in bondage? Ye observe days, and months, and times, and years." It is clear we shouldn't observe birthdays, and in particular, those of religious significance, such as Christmas.

The first time that Christians actually celebrated the birthday of Jesus Christ on December 25th was in Rome in A.D. 336, three hundred years after Jesus Christ died. Aurelian was the emperor of Rome, and he chose the date of December 25th for a pagan festival in Rome to celebrate the birth date of the unconquered sun. December 25th is what is called the winter solstice, the first day that the sun begins to show an

The Making Of A Prophet

increase of light and the days grow longer.

Also, Rome had a festival called Saturnalia that started on December 17th and went through December 24th which was dedicated to Saturn, the god of agriculture and the renewed power of the sun. People exchanged gifts; there was much feasting, drinking, revelry, and orgies.

Because it was such a popular holiday, the church in Rome was not having any success in converting people to its form of Christianity at this time of year. So they took the whole festival and called it "the nativity of the Sun of Righteousness" (from the book of Malachi where Jesus is called the Sun of Righteousness). They publicly proclaimed December 25th as the birthday of the sun; that is, the Son of God, Jesus Christ.

In the eastern part of the empire, this date was not accepted until the fifth century. The church at Jerusalem did not accept December 25th as the date of the birth of Christ until the sixth century when they were forced to by the Pope.

We know too, from the scriptures, that Christ was born much earlier in the fall: "And it came to pass that in those days there went out a decree from Caesar Augustus, that all the world should be taxed, ...and all went to be taxed, everyone into his own city. And Joseph also went up from Galilee, out of the city of Nazareth into Judaea, unto the city of David, which is called Bethlehem;...to be taxed with Mary, his espoused wife, being great with child." (Luke 2:1-5) The Roman emperor would not have made this tax date in the middle of winter. Jesus spoke about the wintertime in Matthew 24:20: "But pray ye that your flight be not in the winter, neither on the Sabbath day." He confirmed that they had hard winters.

Luke 2:8: "And there were in the same country shepherds abiding in the field, keeping watch over their flocks by night." We know, historically, that it was the custom to put the sheep into sheep pens in winter because of the cold. Jesus Christ couldn't have been born in December because the Bible says that the shepherds were abiding in the field, watching over their flocks by night.

If you are wondering whether these issues matter all that much, then consider this: Can God, being holy and perfect, honor a lie? No. Yet some might argue that the Bible says God looks upon the heart. In other words, what matters is the quality of love an individual Christian expresses to God at Christmas. While this may be true, I still believe Christians celebrating Christmas and Easter and even their own birthdays, was never God's Plan A but His Plan B. The Bible also says we should worship God in spirit and in truth and Easter and Christmas are *not* the truth.

Another serious error churches teach, and Christians have swallowed, is that Sunday is the Lord's day, the Sabbath that God commanded to be observed in the fourth commandment. "Remember the Sabbath day to keep it holy." (Exodus 20:8) The Jewish Sabbath, *which Christ observed, please take note*, was from sundown Friday to sundown Saturday, the seventh day of the week. Any encyclopedia will confirm that Sunday is the first day of the week.

But does it really matter which day we keep? Did it matter that Uzzah touched the ark? Did it matter that Samson's hair was cut and that this man of God disobeyed God's seemingly "minor" instructions? If the

The Making Of A Prophet

Ten Commandments are in force today, then yes, it matters! It's amazing that Christians are so proud about keeping the Ten Commandments but so flagrantly violate the fourth.

A second witness to the true seventh day is the historic Christian-professing church. From the early centuries to the present, Christian writers have acknowledged the difference between Sabbath and Sunday, have presented arguments in favor of first-day observance and against seventh-day observance, and have accused Sabbath-keeping Christians of "Judaizing."

The claim that we cannot know for sure which day is the Sabbath is completely fallacious. All the currently popular television evangelists, all biblical historians, and all educated Christian pastors know that Jesus observed the seventh-day Sabbath--the day we call Saturday--the day the Jews have always observed.

In Ezekiel 20:12,13, God says: "Moreover I also gave them my Sabbaths, to be a sign between them and me, that they might know that I am the Lord who sanctifies them. Yet the house of Israel rebelled against me in the wilderness; they did not walk in my statutes; they despised my judgments...and they greatly defiled my Sabbaths. Then I said I would pour out my fury on them in the wilderness, to consume them."

Did it matter that Israel polluted God's Sabbath? God says, "So I also raised my hand in an oath to them in the wilderness, that I would not bring them into the land which I had given them, 'flowing with milk and honey,' the glory of all lands." (Verse 15)

Why did God threaten to refuse His people entry into the promised land? "Because they despised my judgments and did not walk in my statutes, but *profaned my Sabbaths*; for their hearts went after their idols." (Verse 16)

Some believe that the fourth commandment is not among the "moral aspects" of the law--that only those commandments that have to do with love are important to the Christian. But what is love? And how do we express love toward God? In Exodus 20:6, God's mercy is promised to "thousands, to those who love (Him) and keep (His) commandments." Notice the connection between love and commandment keeping. This concurs fully with 1 John 5:3: "For this is the love of God, that we keep His commandments."

While love toward God certainly does involve human emotion, it is expressed first and foremost in obedience to Him. Jesus said, "If you love me, (you will) keep my commandments." (John 14:15) Our obedience to God's law, then, directly reflects the love we have for Him.

Christians who keep the seventh-day Sabbath are often thought to be "a little strange." Sabbath-keeping churches are often labeled "cults." Seldom does one find in a Christian bookstore material promoting Sabbath observance. Literature against Sabbath keeping is far more common. Yet, James writes: "For whoever shall keep the whole law, and yet stumble in one point, he is guilty of all. For He who said, 'Do not commit adultery,' also said, 'Do not murder.' Now if you do not commit adultery, but you do murder, you have become a transgressor of the law." (James 2:10,11)

The prophet Isaiah gives us good reason to believe that the Sabbath covenant will continue into the Millennium. Speaking of that period, he writes, "'And it shall

The Making Of A Prophet

come to pass that from one new moon to another, and from one Sabbath to another, all flesh shall come to worship before me,' says the Lord" (Isaiah 66:23)

The phrase "all flesh" indicates that Israel as well as the gentile nations will be keeping the Sabbath. This concurs with Zechariah's prophecy concerning the same period. The prophet writes, "And it shall come to pass that everyone who is left of all the nations which came against Jerusalem shall go up from year to year to worship the King, the Lord of hosts, and to keep the Feast of Tabernacles." (Zechariah 14:16)

These two prophecies positively confirm that all nations will observe God's weekly and annual Sabbaths during the Millennium. How can anyone claim that these observances are not for Christians today? There are 149 scripture verses concerning God's Sabbath and us. Do you think He may have been trying to make a point?

The force behind changing the Lord's day to Sunday was the Catholic church. The emperor Constantine brought pagan sun god worship into the faltering Christian church around 320 A.D. This new law brought Christian, Jew, and Roman pagans under one iron rule--Sunday, the pagan day of the sun, and the Catholic church, to this day, has been the biggest perpetuator of this error.

In the Pope's 1998 encyclical letter to the world he stated, "It's time for all to faithfully restore the sanctity of the Sunday Sabbath; it's time for the world to keep it holy. All nations must establish laws making Sunday the universal day of worship, and all violators (will) be treated as heretics!" Not "should," but "will" be treated as heretics! That should alarm anyone. In the future, anyone who will not observe Sunday as the Lord's day will be persecuted as the world church headed by the Pope initiates a *one-world religion*.

Here you have a blatant attempt to force man to overtly and collectively drive against the commanded law of God. Satan has carefully and masterfully, over time, mostly through the use of the Roman Catholic church system and its Protestant daughters, diverted Christians away from their original and commanded roots.

In November of 1999, Lutheran church officials finally agreed to rejoin hands with Rome, and Billy Graham publicly stated, "We need a one-world unified religion, and Pope John Paul is the best suited to lead the way; he's a great moral leader." Robert Schuller stated at his Crystal Cathedral, "It's time that America return home; it's time that we go back to our mother Rome."

Satan has cleverly keyed on certain prophetic doctrines and manipulated men down through the ages to slightly alter the meaning and perception of these doctrines. He has subliminally converted men's minds to shift us away from God's covenant. Only a small remnant have remained faithful to God's Plan A in all aspects of their lives, and in return, have been given the wisdom to open and rightly understand these time-sealed prophesies. "And I heard another voice from heaven saying, 'Come out of her my people, that you be not partakers of her sins, and that you receive not of her plagues.'" (Revelation 18:3) After you receive this knowledge you are required to act on it, to come out of the perverted *whore* system!

FOURTEEN

AS SO OFTEN HAPPENS IN FAMILIES, much of what I believe has not been embraced by *all* of my children. Once when my teenage grandson, Nick, was visiting I told him I believed that hell had several levels of torment and that the devil had reserved the hottest for drug companies and doctors who have not done right by their patients because of filthy lucre. He stormed out of the house and consequently I'm on a campaign to prove to him the truth of what I said.

The question remains will he accept the various articles I send him as worth his further investigation on this and other subjects or is he, already, so brainwashed by the world system that he is unreachable?

I call myself a reluctant warrior for God, but warrior I am, make no mistake. I've learned a lot about Satan's tactics through the years. Apparently I am on his "hit" list. He seems to know my weaknesses, my strengths; he at times has stolen my joy, killed my enthusiasm, tarnished my testimony. I don't fear him but I do respect what he can do if I get careless.

In my opinion, Christians get attacked for three reasons: (1) They are effective for the Kingdom. (2) They, like sheep, deliberately break out of God's protective corral and are attacked by wolves (demons). (3) They don't believe God's Word. They may blissfully perform their religious obligations year after year working for God, but not *with* Him, but they ignore the promptings of the Holy Spirit. They carry the Gillette translation of the Bible, you know, cutting out the scriptures they can't handle with a razor blade.

Why am I still at it after 70 years of age? And why does God use me in spite of my sometimes rebellion and occasional anger? The answers are not easy coming--God is God and He will have His way.

I don't receive prophetic visions as some do, but I have to admit I do a lot of proclaiming and have a confrontational-type ministry (in case you haven't noticed) which is typical of *all* the prophets in the Bible. The fact that I dislike my ministry is another throwback to prophets of old who often argued with God, very unhappy with what he called them to do.

After struggling with my ministry for years, I received some insight one night when I heard Texe Marrs on shortwave. Texe has to be a prophet (though he never claims it) because of the many truths he has been given and the way he confronts the *beast* government and organized religion. One day he said to the Lord, "Lord, why did you pick me to do this hard ministry?" And the Lord answered, *Because I knew you would do it*. Wow!

I once phoned one of the brothers who hold up the John 3:16 signs at sports events and wasn't surprised to hear that few understood his ministry, not even his wife. He's had a cold beer poured down the back of his neck more than once. Like the apostle's office, few Christians understand the prophet's, in fact, most pas-

The Making Of A Prophet

tors who have sat under dispensational teaching probably fear the prophet more than any of the five-fold ministries. No, I don't relish the handle of prophet for I know what the prophets had to endure because of their big mouths, especially when they came against the religious establishment.

I have studied other present day "watchmen on the wall" who have been warning America of her not-too-distant downfall. Dave Wilkerson is one of these. He wrote a book called *The Vision* in 1977 predicting many events which have since occurred. Another is James Loyd who uses shortwave radio as outreach, as does Brother Stair, who in spite of personal problems, is adamant that Jesus Christ is coming soon. There are many others, probably as many as there are pastors in America. Most of these men (and women) are not aware they are prophets at all but just feel called to preach the Gospel, or like Alex Jones of Austin, Texas, to expose those in our government and the world who have an agenda to trash our Constitution and make all Americans slaves.

Prophets began to be noticed in the 1980s, proclaiming warnings to a sinful society and announcing the soon return of Jesus Christ. When the Bible was written it did not eliminate the need of the prophetic voice of God, but intensified it. The prophet Joel was speaking of the end times when he proclaimed "I will pour out my Spirit in those days, and your sons and daughters shall prophesy." The true prophet cannot add or subtract from the Bible but brings illumination and application of the Word to his generation. He is also to edify, exhort, and comfort the Church. (1 Corinthians 14:3) But most people, it seems, will not take time to hear God who is anxious to speak to us but will not shout to be heard over the noise of our televisions or busy schedules.

Just as John the Baptist prepared the way for Christ's first coming, now a company of prophets has been raised up to prepare the way for Christ's second coming. This sizable group will come forth in the power and spirit of Elijah just before the Messiah appears. And just as John the Baptist (who the religious scribes and theologians of the day rejected) was a sign from God that the Messiah was at hand, likewise, the majority of present day denominational ministers will not recognize or heed the warnings of these last-day prophets. But Jesus is rejoicing over the part the prophets are playing in preparing His Church, and when the prophets have finished their ministry, He will be released to descend from Heaven to be eternally united with His bride.

The Church is the bride of Christ and must be properly prepared, clothed, and made ready for her wedding day without spot or wrinkle. God's Plan A is that the five-fold ministry of apostle, prophet, evangelist, pastor, and teacher do just that. (Ephesians 4:11-12)

If a church is to be a hospital for sinners, not a hotel for saints, and become an effective force for good in its community, it must have the different ascension offices and gifts of the Holy Spirit operating. A church that doesn't embrace *all* the five-fold ministries will always be spiritually anemic and unable to fully meet the needs of individuals. And rather than having degrees from great theological institutions, a strong church's elders will have credentials directly from the

The Making Of A Prophet

Holy Ghost; for instance: BA--Born Again! MD--Master of Demons. DOD--Driver Out of Devils. PHD--Past Having Doubts. BHGP--Baptized with Holy Ghost Power!

One of my favorite watchmen on the wall is a friend and great inspiration to me. Because of certain conflicts I can't use his name, but his story is intriguing and another good example of the various steps God takes in *the making of a prophet.*

He was raised a Catholic, was good in sports, and became "All American" in baseball and football in college. In his sophomore year he broke his arm in football practice and told no one for three days. He developed blood poisoning and ended up in a hospital where a doctor told him they might have to amputate. Scared to death, that night he prayed, "God, if you are God, if you'll let me keep my arm I will give you my life." What happened next is best described in his own words:

> I fell asleep. I felt a burden lift off me like a heavy blanket and when I awoke about 45 minutes later there were a couple of doctors in the room. One doctor had my arm in his hand and he was saying, "It's a miracle. The blood poisoning is gone."
>
> I knew God had done it. Interestingly, He didn't heal the break--I had to wear a cast for six to eight weeks--but I knew He had saved my arm and that was the thing I had asked for. When I told God I'd give Him my life I meant it. I began a personal pilgrimage to know Him, but no matter where I turned, it was like He was playing hide and seek.
>
> I felt like the Shulammite woman who in the Songs of Solomon of the Bible, went to search for the Lord and couldn't find Him. I knew our team quarterback

was a born-again Christian and I'd seen the difference in his life so I began to bug him. He tried to answer all my questions and took me to a meeting of The Fellowship of Christian Athletes. I remember that meeting well because Paul Anderson was the speaker, at that time the strongest man in the world. He spoke from Acts, chapter four, that anyone who would not heed the words of the prophet would be destroyed, and the fear of God came on me. After that I started going to those meetings often, and for four months listened to the leader and came to the conclusion that Jesus Christ was either the biggest egotistical, arrogant maniac that ever walked the face of the earth or He was God's son and deserved my complete adoration, worship and obedience. So I made a decision that Jesus Christ was Lord and I was water baptized by immersion. Six months later, I was baptized in the Holy Ghost.

Within three months of my baptism in the Holy Ghost, I and two other guys started preaching on our campus and in the dorms and about 300 people were saved. We began to have weekly meetings with the new converts and these continued all through my college career.

During those years we were exposed to a lot of different things in the body of Christ that really upset us. For instance we would go to a city-wide evangelistic meeting and see all the politics behind stage, which saved kids would go to what church and the fight between pastors for new church members. From then on we became determined to separate ourselves from the mainstream evangelicals. We refused to apply for nonprofit status from the government; we didn't want any of that. Initially, the brethren wanted to put me on salary but I refused. During that time I went behind the Iron Curtain for a couple of months, smuggled Bibles, and saw the way the brethren lived. I was exposed to

The Making Of A Prophet

a brand of Christianity that ruined me. It was like Isaiah, chapter six. I saw the Lord do all kinds of miracles and I came back with a desire to see a return to New Testament practices when Christians come together. We saw our local church system with its one pastor and realized it was not God's order. God always had plurality of leadership. It wasn't a one-man rule and the early church had freedom and liberty. I began to go into extended fasting and prayer and fasted two days a week for ten years in a row and fasted 20 days and sometimes up to 40 days every year for ten years. Over this time God let me see His power, especially in the spirit of prophecy. Little did I realize how unpopular the prophet's ministry is because often he is called to expose sin.

Our body meetings off campus intensified. There were healings. There were demons coming out of people. Our body was made up mostly of college kids so there wasn't a lot of sickness and disease but we did have many miracles. For instance, one night we were in a dorm room and a young guy was sitting on a heavy metal table. After I was done preaching he said, "I defy your God, if he's God, strike me within the next 24 hours." Immediately I prayed, "Father, manifest yourself to this man." And the metal table he was sitting on split right in half and he fell to the floor. This was no card table but heavily constructed. He accepted the Lord that night.

Once we had a witch in a meeting. As we began to worship the Lord she started to vomit and kept it up as we continued worshiping the Lord, and all the demons came out of her. She was completely set free--got saved in the meeting and had a changed life afterward. There were about 20 guys from our football team attending the Fellowship of Christian Athletes' meetings where we elders would visit, and God healed sore limbs and

Ron Rendleman

sprained ankles.

We had a situation on campus where I was preaching the Gospel and a guy came out of the crowd and started beating me up. Everybody in the crowd knew that if I wanted to, I probably could have killed this guy. But because I didn't do anything, just laid there and kept telling him that Jesus loved him, four people watching got saved because they wanted to know what kind of power I had that could constrain me to love this man while he was hitting me. To me, that's the miraculous--that's the power of God.

We began to get a reputation in the city of being different, cultish--some students, when they found Christ dropped out of school, which didn't set well with their parents. We didn't push for this, it would just happen. We water baptized new converts right away. We used pools, lakes--whatever was available. In our desire to see other born-again churches in the area come into the fullness of Christ rather than being contented to be Christian country clubs, we began to visit pastors and testify as to what God was doing in our personal lives and our meetings. The idea being, that they could have the same manifestations. Sometimes we would lovingly confront a pastor God showed us had a particular sin problem. We were almost always totally rejected. Consequently, we elders decided to visit churches to prophesy and confront sin. I mean, some of these churches were looking the other way when it came to homosexualism, adultery, allowing people to easily divorce and remarry, etc.

One day five of us felt led to confront a particular pastor, a proud self-righteous man. He was a manipulator when it came to money, always taking an offering for something. Basically, he laughed at us. We left him peacefully and started fasting the next day. During this fast I received what I truly believe was a leading from

The Making Of A Prophet

the Lord. I asked a sister in the fellowship to bake a multi-layered cake over a foot high, pure white and very pretty. Inside I told her to put rotten fruit and chicken bones. We walked into the pastor's church on a Sunday morning and I carried the cake in front of his congregation and prophesied out of Matthew 23: "Outwardly you appear white, but inwardly you are full of rottenness and dead men's bones." I threw the cake down on the floor just in front of the pulpit and all the insides gushed out. Immediately people began screaming and running out of the church. Several men grabbed me and dragged me out. I didn't resist them. They threw me out into the crowd outside where I landed in a bunch of kids. I caught one little girl and rolled with her. When I picked her up to give her back to her parents I said to the pastor, "You know, we're not your enemies. I've only come here to warn you," and the Pastor punched me hard in the chest but I just looked at him and smiled. I said, "So, this is the love of God from you, huh?" and I turned and walked away.

A week later, I received an affidavit. We were accused of mob action, and ordered to court. I didn't take a lawyer because I was going to tell the truth. I told the judge, who was a Jew and thought we were Hitlerites, "Your Honor, I'm an ex-football player, I took karate, I can lift heavy weights. You mean to tell me if I was going in there for a violent purpose, I would have walked out with only a $50 rug stain and nobody getting hurt? Besides, the truth is, this thing should never have come before the state. It should have been brought before the churches in the area, but the churches are cowardly--they have no ability to confront."

The judge's answer was that older people in the church could have had a heart attack because we had frightened them and our intent was violent. I answered, "Your Honor, our intent was not violence. If I had really intended to do harm, those men could never have dragged me out of there." We five elders each received ten days in jail and a combined fine of $8,000. I was restricted from traveling outside of my town for a period of two-and-a-half years.

While we were in jail, three or four guys were saved. We went home rejoicing. Of course, the local newspapers had a heyday, claiming we were a cult. "Cult" in the dictionary is described as "obsessive devotion or veneration for a person, principle, or ideal." Since we have obsessive devotion to Jesus Christ, I guess you could call us a cult.

Some have asked me, "Looking back, did you do the right thing?" My answer is *yes*. We had fasted and prayed, asking for direction. We were asking in faith and true faith must never waver but must always result in action. But the action must not contradict the scriptures. In our case, our actions were quite supported by numerous examples of prophets' behaviors in coming against the sins of society in their day. Also, all during those years our confidence was continually fed by many signs and wonders that confirmed our ministries, just as Christ promised for any true believer that labored in His name. (Mark 16:17)

I remember one time in 1984 I and a few elders were traveling around the country establishing meetings. We were driving to a meeting near Spokane one winter day when we witnessed a terrible accident--a car right in front of us hit a tree at high speed. I told our driver to pull over and I and another elder ran to the car to find four bloody teens. Someone ran up with a crowbar and we got a door open. I grabbed the nearest kid who was a real mess. His face looked broken and terribly lacerated. I sat down in the snow and held him

The Making Of A Prophet

in my lap, weeping and praying in tongues until an ambulance came and the medics took him from me. The brothers then called me over to another boy laid out on the side of the road. He was also a mess and was obviously unconscious. There were dozens of people around us now. Another brother and I laid hands on the boy and prayed in tongues. Someone in the crowd yelled, "Get those Jesus freaks out of here." But we kept praying until the paramedics tried to revive him. Finally, one of them put a mirror under his nose to see if he was breathing. "He's gone," the medic said. *No*, I said in my spirit. I stood up and shouted, "In the name of Jesus Christ I rebuke the spirit of death!" Immediately, the boy sat up straight--eyes wide open and screamed. Everybody freaked out, including me. I went down on my knees and began to worship God. All four kids were released from the hospital, okay.

Other things happened. The Lord told me to go to four different men, each with gross sin in their lives. I did and none responded to my warnings. Within six months two died, and two became extremely sick. I prophesied the stock market crash in '88, one year before it happened, and a drought the same year. I told the brethren that in 2001 we would see changes in America. On September 7, 2001, we started a five-day fast--on the fourth day of the fast the World Trade Center buildings were destroyed.

God began to awaken me at night. I'd have great pain in several joints of my body. He told me within a few months a big catastrophe would hit America far worse than September 11th. (This is being written May 01, 2003.) Because He is displeased with America, God has lifted His hand of protection from our great country. Recently, President Bush sanctioned gay pride day and allegedly has at least one sodomite in his cabinet.

Ron Rendleman

> The brokenness in my body--hip, knee pain and lack of function is a prophetic picture of the body of Christ. The legalism, the stiffness, the cloistered attitude of churches, all hinder the freedom that's supposed to be in the body of Christ. The scripture says, "He that stiffens his neck after much reproof will suddenly be broken and that beyond remedy." (Proverbs 29:1)
>
> The church age is going out, the Kingdom age is coming in. God will raise up ministries that will restore the body of Christ, with no spot or wrinkle. Tribulation will bring this about. Everything in America that is exalted above God--technology, commerce, stock market, medicine, sports, etc., He will bring down. We will be a crippled America and we will be attacked from abroad--most likely by a nuclear attack.
>
> The Lord will give His remnant wisdom--He will provide for them supernaturally. He will multiply the bread that I might give to my neighbor in famine. If we don't have the faith to believe God for miracles like multiplying bread, etc. then we must fast and pray now to prepare for that day. Jesus said, "When I come will I find faith? Faith, hope and love these three abide--but the greatest of these is love." So faith and love are going to be what separates the remnant from the organized church world. Many will not repent. My prayer is for the remnant. I no longer pray for America, it will be lost.

These are hard words from the prophet, but sometimes it takes strong words and actions to wake up a complacent society that is self indulged and distracted by sensual gratification of unlimited variety.

I believe it was in late 1988 that the Lord first gave me the order that shifted my prophetic ministry into high gear. *Put loudspeakers on your Ramcharger, go to construction sites and announce that I'm coming soon,*

The Making Of A Prophet

I heard in my spirit.

"Lord, I can't do that." I prayed. "I'll get busted. And if that doesn't happen, I'm sure to get a brick through a window!"

It was another "what if" situation. You know, you get an order from the Holy Spirit to make restitution or apologize to someone, something hard to do, and Satan starts with his song and dance--"If you do that, your wife will think less of you, your boss will fire you, etc." Of course, all these predictions never happen, but their purpose is to put severe doubt and fear into you. Sometimes you can't shake it no matter how you pray. The only sure remedy is gritting your spiritual teeth and get the job over with, no matter how painful. God has spoken.

There is another way out, of course. Just harden your heart, pretend not to hear--lose yourself in work, hobbies, or family. I've done that too. But one day you realize the presence of the Lord is no longer with you, and you find yourself doing things you used to do in the old life. So if you care enough, you scamper back to the fold, only to find the gate to the pasture shut and not to be opened until you do what the Lord commanded in the first place.

After I began going to the construction sites around South Elgin, Illinois (and nothing harmful ever happened, just vocal abuse), my next order was to go to the local restaurant and make the same announcement. Again, I fought obedience but gave in after a few days; I just couldn't out-box God.

Again, nothing dreadful happened. Next He told me to visit other restaurants and bars, always with the same message: *Jesus Christ is coming soon*. Although

I've had my share of insults, I've only been manhandled once, by a local businessman. I pressed charges with the local police, but the Lord told me to drop them, that I wasn't in town to make enemies. These restaurants cater to blue collar workers. Since we don't have the town square anymore, these businesses and the shopping malls are where the people are.

One afternoon I walked into a local pub, made my announcement that Christ was coming soon, and a young woman bartender told me to take a hike. Three more times that week the Lord impressed upon me to do the same thing and by this time the gal was livid and threatened to call the cops. Then came the real struggle. *Go and ask the girl that if she were to die tonight, would she go to heaven?*

I couldn't believe what I had heard. This would be a major confrontation. That night I didn't sleep very well. In the morning I called a local Assembly of God pastor whom I respected. After all, the Word speaks of wisdom through counsel of the brothers. "You'll never win anyone to the Lord with actions like that," was all he said.

"Thank you," I sighed. "You just got me off the hook." Or so I thought. As soon as we hung up, the Lord spoke again. *Will you listen to My voice or the voice of man?* So, at twelve noon the next day, I went back, told her I had a question to ask, and when she finally calmed down, I laid it on her.

"That's it, that's it!" she cried and ran for the phone. Sometimes I wait for the police, sometimes not. This time I decided to leave.

After arriving home, sure enough, the phone rang and a South Elgin officer invited me to come down to

The Making Of A Prophet

the station. He was polite and all, and I told him that since I had delivered my message, I wouldn't be returning to the restaurant. I learned later the gal had some drug problems. Two weeks after my visit, the restaurant closed down. The Lord knew.

It reminds me of the time I witnessed in another bar in the same area. I began to know the regulars pretty well and because one of the wives seemed really interested in the Bible, I offered to start a Bible study in the back pool room on Sunday afternoons. We started with two of the wives while their husbands guzzled beer up front. Two weeks after we began, the tavern burned to the ground. Some say it was faulty wiring; I say it was short-circuited by Satan.

The Lord has sent me to many places with the message that He is returning soon. I've been to high school football games, county fairs, shopping malls, flea markets, the Chicago Bears training camp at Platteville, Wisconsin, almost every place people gather in numbers. If I hear about a holiday parade I usually manage to drive down the parade route 15 minutes before the parade starts and am able to reach a lot of people with the truck's loudspeakers.

I was pulled over while preaching in St. Charles, Illinois, in the summer of '92 by an officer who didn't know the law. Year's ago in Saia vs. NY, the Supreme Court ruled that "cities cannot ban loud speakers, or censor annoying ideas, and that no police officer should make persons lose time in court to prove a right which is already theirs." Many local ordinances violate our constitutional rights. Of course, I try to be wise and not wake up a neighborhood at four in the morning.

One experience I had taught me much about what

God thinks of His Word. For about a month the Lord sent me into a fancy restaurant at noon where the local businessmen gathered. They had a rather large main room so I would slip by the hostess and walk into the middle of the floor and say in a strong voice, "Attention, attention please, Jesus Christ is coming soon." I tried to look pleasant and then I would head for the exit, pronto. Sometimes, I would say, "I have some good news and some bad news. The good news is that Jesus Christ is coming soon. The bad news is that no one is ready."

Things started getting tense. The management was not happy. I began to plead with the Lord for relief from this unpleasant task. And I mean plead. And then all at once, a verse came to me, Matthew 10:14. "And whoever does not receive you, nor heed your words as you go out of that house or that city, shake the dust off your feet."

The next morning I drove right to the place. Stopping at the front door, I got out, stamped my feet on the pavement "shaking off the dust," and I said to the Lord, "Lord, I stand on that verse right now because they won't receive your message." And wonderfully, my burden to preach there lifted, never to return. While my pleadings were ignored, standing on His Word was not.

What will happen to those who reject you? This is what the Lord told me about that. One fine day I was standing at Chicago's State and Madison. They used to call it the busiest crossroads in the world. I had a thousand tracts and was passing them out when I noticed that an abnormally large number were being thrown away. It began to get to me. Finally, I prayed,

The Making Of A Prophet

"Father, what's happening? Most of them don't want these tracts." *You are being used as a judgment tool,* He answered. *Someday you will be a witness against those who refuse me.*

I understood a lot more then about how God would deal with the lost. Always fair, He will bring to remembrance to those who ignored His plan of salvation, every refused tract, every turned off gospel message on the radio or TV, every blaspheme against His servants. It reinforced what I had learned earlier, that I was just an errand boy, if the message was rejected it wasn't my concern--I had done my job. I had been obedient. Most people I witness to are Christ rejecters. I cannot change that, nor feel remorse. I must faithfully search out the few in the mob whom God knows are ready to be saved. Even Jesus didn't pray for the world. At the last supper in John 17:9 He prayed, "I pray for them (the apostles): I pray not for the world, but for them which Thou hast given Me." How about that?

One day the Lord told me to visit a local church on Sunday morning and at an appropriate time, like when the collection is taken, stand up and tell the congregation of His soon return. It was hard, but I did it and moved on to other churches in the town. After the first few, I had real doubts because of the lack of positive response and the spirit of oppression I felt. I needed encouragement so I called three men of God who knew me well and whom I respected. Not one of them was encouraging. They thought I was in the flesh and was being disruptive. You can imagine how I felt then. Still, I was being pushed to give the same message. Sometimes I would call a pastor in advance, but this wasn't what the Lord wanted because when I did, the answer was always the same: "Come to our Wednesday night meeting for testimony time." The problem with that is there would probably be 15 people present. The Lord wanted me to address the whole church. You'd think I was asking for an hour of time. I always told the pastors exactly what I would say--one sentence--but *not one* ever invited me.

How many times have I sat in a service very uneasy because I knew the Lord wanted me to stand up. I would pray, "Lord, just have the pastor ask, 'does anyone have anything to share?'" But it very seldom happens because most pastors are control freaks, hopelessly caught up in tradition, deathly afraid of the unexpected...how sad because the body of Christ suffers for it.

I was ushered out of a service one Wednesday evening and it opened my eyes to see how far some well known "born again" churches are from New Testament order. The church was Willowcreek, located in wealthy Barrington, Illinois.

The Lord had spoken to me in the morning about going there that night and to make the usual announcement. I fought it at first, but then reasoned that a Wednesday night prayer meeting shouldn't be intimidating. Little did I know, their prayer meeting was a "community sing" consisting of about 3,000 people, seated in a modern amphitheater. "Okay, Lord. You've got to be kidding." I prayed. My first thought was to go up front and find a live mike. I would simply make my announcement before the service, nice and clean, no hassle. No such luck. The service began with a large choir leading the singing and when they finally

The Making Of A Prophet

left the stage, one of the pastors (they had several) came out and announced he would preach from Genesis. He called the church to prayer and I knew that was my opportunity. When he finished his prayer, I was standing in the center isle, 15 feet away looking up at him.

"Pastor, with your permission," I began, and turned around to the audience proclaiming loudly, "Ladies and gentlemen, Jesus Christ sent me here tonight to tell you that He is coming soon, much sooner than anyone thinks."

At that moment two men appeared out of nowhere and took me out. The audience was dead silent. You would think that at least a few brave souls would have yelled "amen," impulsively, like what happens sometimes in a restaurant when I preach. When we were almost to the foyer, the pastor said over the microphone, "Satan will do anything to disrupt a service!"

I couldn't believe my ears. He was accusing me of being a spokesman for the evil one. My spirit was burning but I tried to maintain composure. I was friendly to the six or seven security men, with their walkie-talkies, surrounding me in the foyer and told them they had nothing to fear, I was leaving.

When I finally found my car, two Barrington policemen walked up to me.

"What's your problem?" one asked.

"Well, if you're born again, I will answer you one way, if you're not, I will answer another way. Are you?"

"Yes," one answered.

"Okay, do you believe Jesus is coming soon?"

"Yes I do," he said firmly.

"Then what's wrong with me telling those people in there that?"

"Well...you caused a disruption, they didn't like it."

"Look, I can't help that, I'm just an errand boy." I went on to tell them that I didn't just escape from nearby Elgin State Mental Hospital, that I was a successful businessman and when I finished with all the prophecies that have been fulfilled, they didn't have much to say.

For the next couple of days I couldn't forget the pastor's words. I sat down and wrote him a long letter of explanation in which I made this statement, "...Pastor, I believe the Lord is upset with the cloistered attitude of pastors today and that's why He had me speak from your floor. Can you honestly say you would have allowed me to address your church if I had called you first?" (He later admitted on the phone that he would not have.) "But pastor, we have a slight problem, is it possible that you over reacted to me and attributed to Satan what the Holy Spirit had ordained, therefore nullifying God's message to the people? If you agree that you spoke hastily, would you consider speaking to the people at next Wednesday's service and tell them that though you may not agree with my methods, what I said was not wrong, that Jesus Christ is coming soon?" Two days later I received a phone call from the pastor and it was obvious I had his attention; he was afraid I'd show up at next Wednesday's service.

We got into it a bit. I told him his church service wasn't scriptural and I quoted 1 Corinthians 14:26. "How is it then brethren? When you come together every one of you has a psalm, a doctrine, a tongue, a

The Making Of A Prophet

revelation, an interpretation. Let all things be done unto edifying...if anything be revealed to another that sits by, let the first one hold his peace. For you may all prophesy one by one, that all may learn, and all may be comforted."

His answer was that at the end of the chapter it said, "Let all things be done decently and in order," that I was not in order by speaking out. I was stumped for a short time till I realized his order wasn't God's order. I had not violated God's order at all since asking his permission to speak wasn't even scriptural, but a courtesy gesture. But on the phone with him, the Lord led me to say "Pastor, I'll make a deal."

"I don't make deals," he retorted.

"Here's the deal, if you'll read Matthew 10:14 to your elders, I won't be back. 'And whosoever shall not receive you nor hear your words when you depart out of that house or city, shake the dust off your feet... verily I say unto you, it shall be more tolerable for Sodom and Gomorrah in the day of judgment, than for that city.'"

"It's a deal," he finally said quietly. Now get this, no sooner had I hung up the phone when the Lord said, *Now, call him back and tell him that he must read your letter to all the elders.*

I couldn't believe it. But I couldn't get peace. Some of you who read this will know exactly what I mean, many of you won't. When I called him back he readily agreed. Whether he did or not was not my concern.

Every church has its critics and Willowcreek has had its share. Do I feel that God has used Willowcreek and its satellite churches to touch souls? Absolutely. Do they preach the soon return of Jesus Christ? Not often enough, according to some. Do I feel they follow Biblical worship in their services? If they had, they wouldn't have ushered me out. But they are not alone, most churches in America don't. And because these churches are not led by the Holy Spirit, they are anemic and powerless. Little wonder they don't have the courage to speak out against sins like abortion or tyrannical acts of the government.

I believe in the critical times fast approaching, a great number of Christian organizations and churches throughout the world will be phased out of God's master plan. They may continue to operate on self-generated business power, but they won't have the anointing.

In fact, many of them will rush to be part of the soon-to-appear one-world ecumenical religion headed by the Pope in Rome, and they will actively persecute the true bride of Christ who refuse to partake of their idolatry. In recent years I've met an ever-increasing number of Christians who relate how God told them to leave their church. Interestingly, they almost always quote Revelation 18:4-5, "Then I heard another voice from heaven say: 'Come out of her, my people, so that you will not share in her sins, so that you will not receive any of her plagues; for her sins are piled up to heaven, and God has remembered her crimes.'"

The great whore is the *beast*-sanctioned whore of Babylon of Revelation--part of which is the commercial religion of Christianity, Incorporated. Unless Willowcreek and other "born again" 501(c)(3) churches repent and depart from the great Babylonian mother of harlots, their candlesticks will be removed and Christ will spew them out of His mouth.

The Making Of A Prophet

How did these churches sink to such a despicable godless form of religion? It was a long gradual process, and it must be tearfully admitted to be one of the crown jewels in Satan's accomplishments. But just as he used medical schools to corrupt young doctors to believe drugs were the only answer to a patient's problems, Satan used Dallas Theological Seminary, Moody Bible Institute, Bob Jones University, and seminaries to corrupt young ministers with dispensational theology. It shouldn't come as a shock that his attack against the Church began centuries ago.

Let me explain: Around the third century, the Roman Empire, realizing it could not eliminate Christianity, adopted it. The purpose, of course, was to put Christians in subjection. One of the most seemingly harmless, but devastatingly effective changes, was the replacement of the scriptural pattern of worship in the book of Acts and the Epistles by a control system of providing a building where people didn't face each other, but sat row behind row. Hopefully, there must have been some Christians who met together privately for pure worship of God, but the "breaking of bread from house to house daily" in Acts 2:46 and spontaneous interaction of I Corinthians 14:26-31 obviously was not encouraged and gradually died off.

The openness and willingness to exchange with one another, to build one another up, is painfully absent in Rome's system of "church" where celebration of the Mass replaces scriptural worship and fellowship. Other teachings were: that only Rome had the key to unlock the Holy Scriptures, that man-made church dogma was equal to scripture. Also, indulgences, purgatory, celibacy, abstinence of certain foods, priests as mediators who held the power to turn wine and bread into the blood and body of our Lord, Mariolatry, and worship of saints all worked to keep Christians in bondage. Self-sacrifice and good works guaranteed heaven, replacing faith in Jesus Christ as being complete in itself for salvation. Baptism, an act that Christ commanded of His repentant followers, was interpreted as a "works" requirement that even parents could practice to help pave the way to a heavenly place for their infant children.

But one of the most significant facts not widely realized by Christians today is that though Martin Luther and other reformation fathers recognized the correct basis of salvation, the importance of scripture, and the many unscriptural doctrines of Rome, they seemingly missed a very important truth. Had they preached an uncompromising return to scripture, the body of Christ would have experienced restoration instead of reformation. Evidently, they did not realize how very vital to spiritual life the original five-fold ministry practiced by the early assemblies was.

It is obvious from searching the scriptures that New Testament church meetings were free wheeling and full of expression and that they accomplished three things: (1) to worship God in spirit and in truth; (2) to learn God's Word (and not always in a lecture delivered by the pastor every week); (3) to meet the needs of those present.

Ask yourself honestly, does your church meet these requirements? Are you free to stand in a Sunday morning service to share your burden, your joy? Do you feel lonely and unimportant in church and feel the service would be exactly the same without you? As James Rutz so aptly puts it..."In the early church, God was the audience and the worshippers were the performers. But today the pastor is the performer, and we're the audience...fellowship is confined to the foyer afterward, please. Try to speak and the ushers will 'ush' you out."

What gives a body meeting life are the gifts--not talents--gifts: prophecy, tongues, interpretation, doctrine of truth, revelation, etc., all expressions of a living Christ to meet the needs of everyone present. The root word for gift is "charisma." This comes from the word "char" which means joy. "Charis" is the word grace, which God gives us to accomplish His will. Interestingly, have you ever noticed the churches who preach against the gifts are usually the most joyless?

But God desires for us to function in our gifts and is pleased when we seek the best of them. (I Corinthians 12:31) It is possible to have all of them, as Paul did. God is no respecter of persons and I believe the gifts will be most manifested in an assembly when the majority present have had the baptism with the Holy Spirit.

If you have trouble determining your gifts, especially for ministry, check your motivation. If you were allowed to do only one thing for God for the rest of your life, what would it be? Prophecy? Serve others? Teach? Exhort (stimulating the faith of others)? Giving? Ruling (organizing God's work)? Mercy (comforting those in distress)? (Romans 12:5)

If you're still unsure, ask yourself these questions: Do I have any unresolved problems in my life--have I made peace with every man? How involved am I with the lives of others? How much am I in tune to the needs of others? How much do I imitate other ministries rather than look to God for the unique ministry He has waiting for me?

All over America, and abroad, informal home prayer meetings or house fellowships have emerged--God's answer to many hungry hearts to prepare them for the chaos to come. Some cities reportedly have over a thousand. No one but God can know how many of these meetings there are all over the world.

But sometimes a group of Christians will come out of deadness, begin their own house church and for awhile everything is great--the Spirit is really present. But then that fresh breath they received stagnates into a deadness just as great as what they fled from because they get more comfortable with what God has done than what He wants to do *now*.

Leadership in the New Testament church was plural. One strong reason the church is weak today is that so many pastors have tried to be the shepherd, teacher, evangelist--Jack of all trades, master of none. Jesus poured His life into twelve men only; today's pastors try to lead two or three hundred and sometimes thousands and wonder why so little fruit is born.

Some pastors say, "I know all that is true but what can I do about it? I'm trapped by the traditions of my church." I feel if every man will try to live God's Word and obey it, and not let the fear of man rule his heart, God will show him the way.

Many pastors are in no position to disciple anyone--their wives are not submissive, their children are rebellious, their followers spiritual babes. I have found you can preach tremendous sermons to a flock but you will reproduce what you are. A pastor's first disciples are his wife and children.

The Making Of A Prophet

In a day when a former God-fearing nation has turned to many forms of idol worship--where immorality is skyrocketing, the great body of believers who are called the salt of the earth, who once made such an impression that it was said of them "they turned the world upside down," are still practicing a twice-removed form of Romish tradition in their churches that has a form of Godliness but denies the power thereof, is sadly ineffective, and can only reproduce stillbirths.

Yes, Satan has done his job well and today most churches in America are under his control. Oh, he will let them have their worship time, their prayer time, their preaching time, in fact, he will see to it so well that it becomes a tradition stamped in concrete. If you don't believe it, try to change it. Church attendance is at an all-time high; church buildings are going up more beautiful and spacious than ever, yet Christians are increasingly sadly ineffective--practicing a form of godliness but denying the power therein, and that's what's known as religion. Richard Jolly puts it this way...

> When you know Jesus Christ, really know Him, you will be free and no religion will be able to control you. A religion is what a religious demon has people do for him. That is, every religion has a name and that name is the name of a religious demon which demands that men worship it. "What say I then? That the idol (temple or religion) is anything, or that which is offered in sacrifice to idols is anything? But I say, that the things which the nations sacrifice, they sacrifice to demons, and NOT TO GOD: and I would not that you should have fellowship with demons." (I Corinthians 10:19-20) The idols used to be called Baalim, Jupiter, Mercury, Diana, etc. Today demons are called Catholic, Baptist,

Pentecostal, Evangelical or whatever. They are good-sounding names of religious demons. "You cannot drink the cup of the Lord, and the cup of demons: you cannot be partakers of the Lord's table, and of the table of demons." (I Corinthians 10:22-23)

Denominations work with earthly things. They build temples and other idols. They ask for money for their earthly works. They have their books and schools for teaching their ways, and their laws and customs consist of earthly rituals. Satan lies to men and says that all this is necessary: "Without a temple where are men going to gather to worship God?" The Lord, Jesus Christ says, "Believe me, the hour comes when you will neither in this mountain, nor even at Jerusalem worship: for salvation is of the Jews. But the hour comes, and now is, when the true worshippers shall worship the Father in spirit and in truth for the Father seeks such to worship Him. God is Spirit: and they that worship Him must worship Him in spirit and in truth." (John 4:21-24)

Jesus Christ says explicitly that it is necessary to worship God in spirit and in truth, not in one certain place nor in another, nor does it do any good to worship even in Jerusalem which is the capital of the so-called "Christian" religions. There isn't any place: the Spirit doesn't have a fixed location! Hallelujah! Thank God! And therefore, because the true Church of Jesus Christ is in the Spirit, "the gates of hell will not prevail against her." (Matthew 16:18) The Spirit of God dwells in the saints. Men in their religions worship what they don't know: they think of God but they see only the temples and all the religious paraphernalia, through which man can never know god.

Religious leaders take the offerings, tithes and works of sinners and build a building, a temple, and when it's completed, they stupefy ignorant men by saying "here is your house of God," and men enter in that temple, as if in truth that it is the sanctuary or residence of God. But God says, "Heaven is my throne, and the earth is my footstool. What house will you build me?" says the Lord, or "What is the place of my rest? Has not My hand made all the things?" (Acts 7:49-50) "Know you not that YOU are the temple of god, and that the Spirit of God dwells in you?" (I Corinthians 3:16)

Presently religions are enjoying their financial businesses and all their activity is based upon money. Everything for them has its center in the offerings and tithes and around the money table. They don't conduct any service without asking for and expecting money. This is natural, since they are businesses of this world, their "ministers" are hirelings--without money they cannot do anything, because everything they do is of this world, whose activities and work are based upon money.

These words may be hard to accept from Richard Jolly, but I feel he is right on. In my street work through the years, I've heard a lot of criticism of churches and TV evangelists who beg for money or sell books, trinkets, prayer cloths, tapes, even prophecies given to them by God which are passed on to the saints in exchange for a "love offering" (of $29.95 for a VCR tape, thank you very much). True, many ministries can point to thousands who have found the Lord through them, but only because Christ's absolute highest priority is reaching the lost, in spite of all the excess baggage that must truly grieve Him.

Over the years through compromise and taking the easy road, too many ministers have become politically correct but spiritually bankrupt. Instead of preaching against sin and corruption in government they preached about heaven. Their flocks, instead of becoming Christ's army against the enemy, became so heavenly minded they are no earthly good. It is totally illogical that God's desire is that His people be separated from day-to-day civil activities and government, which have such a great effect on every citizen. As the years passed, America sank ever deeper into immoral excess and government corruption and the great majority of Christian leaders in the country were continually silent.

For instance, where were Robert Shuller, Paul Crouch, or Billy Graham and other TV preachers when the FBI burned down the Branch Davidian complex in Waco and told a pack of lies to cover their sins? Pat Robertson and Jerry Falwell, to their credit, did speak out and Falwell distributed the "Clinton Chronicles" film that makes Clinton out to be a murderer.

Christians need to understand that their television ministry, their little corner church, their publishing company, could be the next to come under the scrutiny of the *beast* government. I don't agree with the doctrines of Jehovah Witnesses, Mormons, or the Branch Davidians at Waco, but the Constitution guarantees their right to exist, and so must I.

One reason the Christian church in America muzzled itself into silence was because it let the IRS replace Jesus Christ as head of His Church. It probably began in the 1930s when the IRS said to pastors, "We have some goodies for you. You can get housing and automobile allowances. Just sign here." So the preachers lined up to drink at the trough, and hardly anyone spoke out against it. Today, churches and Christian organizations are all 501(c)(3) and they don't dare preach against sodomites, abortionists, state lotteries, even pornography. If they do, they lose their tax exemption.

They always use Romans 13 to defend total obedience to government, forgetting that Paul wrote that letter to the Romans from prison and did not preach blanket submission to government. Government is accountable to God. But when a government orders us to do something that goes against God's law, we are no longer obligated to obey. God is not happy that it's now lawful to be a homosexual or that it's now lawful to steal, just as long as you do it by Congress, or that it's legal to murder a baby, just do it before it's born, and by latest statistics, in some of the larger cities, more babies are aborted than born--50 million of them since Roe vs. Wade. So, should I blindly support the government with my tax money and never take a stand against its unGodly actions? I don't think so. In fact, the Bible orders me to stand against evil. It orders me to be the salt of the earth. Salt is a preserver, but it's also an irritant.

Those so-called ministers of God who conveniently hide behind Romans 13, either to defend their subservience to the IRS or not speaking out against an oppressive government, usually have nothing to say when confronted with Revelation 13:16-17: "And he (the *beast* government) caused all, both small and great, rich and poor, free and bond to receive a mark (biochip) in their right hand or in their foreheads and that no man might buy or sell save he have the mark or the name of the *beast* or the number of his name." That number is 666. And by the way, in the Hebrew alphanumeric code, 666 is WWW or World Wide Web, (said the spider to the fly).

Will these ministers, these wolves in sheep's clothing who have come to destroy, who are so careful to obey the government, tell their flocks that they must hurry down to the post office Saturday morning to be injected with their very own high-tech, state-of-the-art computer identity chip because the government orders it? Of course they will because they're obeying the government, rather than God, right now. And because of them, many of their flocks will be destroyed. Just remember Revelation 14:9-10: "...If any man worship the *beast* and his image and receive his mark in his forehead or in his hand, the same shall drink of the wine of the wrath of God which is poured out without mixture into the cup of his indignation and he shall be tormented with fire and brimstone in the presence of the holy angels and in the presence of the Lamb."

Another thought concerning Romans 13. The verse states: "Let every soul be subject unto the higher powers for there is no power but of God, the powers that be are ordained of God." But who are the powers in America? Are they Congress, or the President, or the Supreme Court judges? It might come as a surprise to you, but *you* and *I* are the powers in America--**we the people**--are the sovereigns in America. According to the supreme law of the land, the Constitution, all our public servants, from the President down to the traffic cop are all subject unto the people. America is very different from other countries in this respect, especially Rome which was the *power* in authority when Paul wrote Romans 13.

These Roman 13 advocates have also told their flocks there will be a rapture of Christians before the

The Making Of A Prophet

great tribulation. "Not to worry," they say to their people. God will take you out of here in the nick of time so that you won't be left behind to suffer with the rest of the world. But in my thinking, this is a great deception that has given Christians a "comfy" blanket-- a false sense of security. I'm amused at my friend, Jerry Jenkins, who became a multimillionaire writing the *Left Behind* novels that were based on this false doctrine.

One may point to the converts who were reached with books like these and argue that therein lies the proof that the rapture doctrine is true. I have two thoughts to offer: (1) It is impossible to know how many of these "converts" were brought to the true Christ. Did their emotional "happening" with time, vaporize, leaving them unchanged, unrepentant? (2) I have known several cases where people were moved toward God by a TV special or reading a novel that was based on half truths. My opinion is that Jesus will use any and all we offer Him to reach the lost--the reason He came and sacrificed Himself in the first place. But it is not proof that the vehicle used to touch someone is errorless.

They tell me the Christians in China became embittered with their rapture-teaching pastors when they saw the communists bash their babies' heads against the wall. "You told us we would not go through suffering like this, that Jesus would come in time to spare us this tribulation," they accused their ministers.

The word, "rapture" cannot be found in the Bible, nor was the doctrine believed or preached by Christians until eighteen hundred years after Christ. In the early nineteenth century a young girl supposedly had a direct word from Christ. A few pastors began to preach the doctrine and by the 1900s with the help of Darby, Scoffield, and other big-name evangelicals, the doctrine became "gospel." This is a classic example of how Christians can be hoodwinked into believing a false doctrine because of their laziness in not searching the Bible for truth.

There are dozens of verses that discredit the rapture teaching and we won't list them, but I must call your attention to Matthew, Chapter 24. Jesus is speaking to his disciples and warns them of the "beginning of sorrows." He speaks of pestilences, earthquakes, great persecution of the saints, great immorality in the world..."immediately after the tribulation of those days shall the sun be darkened, and the moon shall not give her light, and the stars shall fall from heaven, and the powers of the heavens shall be shaken; and *then* shall appear the sign of the Son of Man in heaven; and *then* shall all the tribes of the earth mourn, and they shall see the Son of Man coming in the clouds of heaven with power and great glory." Notice the number of conditions that must be met. Yet, the rapture people insist that Christ will return for His remnant before all these signs take place. I believe this diabolical doctrine must make Satan quite proud. With it, he has yet another tool to keep the Church blissfully happy and unconcerned. After all, why worry about preparing for a great tribulation if you're going to escape it through a secret rapture?

That American Christians have become complacent, gullible and easily deceived is born out by Harold Rosenthal's words. He was an assistant to Senator Javit back in 1976. He said his people were amazed how

The Making Of A Prophet

easily American Christians can be manipulated to submit to their every demand. His staff used the churches, the news media, and economic institutions to control those he called religious puppets. Why were they puppets? Because they blindly followed blind shepherds. I'm reminded of the old saying, "If a man doesn't stand for something, he will fall for anything."

FIFTEEN

WE HAVE A TAX REBELLION IN AMERICA. The IRS doesn't want you to know there are at least 50 million protesters in a fast-growing movement that are sick of working almost half a year for the government. While there is a good percentage who just want to have more money to spend, I feel a large number of these protesters are just tired of being slaves. County and state taxes are lawful, for the most part, but taxing personal income is absolutely unlawful. More on that later.

The IRS, with the help of the government, has schemed to bring all Christian churches under its total control. It has done this by convincing the pastors that they had to incorporate under 501(c)(3). Overnight, pastors became tax collectors, even informers on their own people, because they feared the IRS more than God, Almighty.

One brave pastor, who in 1987 realized he had been deceived and had made the IRS head of his church and repented of it, is Gregory J. Dixon of the Indianapolis Baptist Temple in Indiana. While he never told his flock not to pay personal taxes, he was adamant about not being a tax collector for the IRS and collect taxes from those who ministered in the church. In his words, "There are no limits to the First Amendment which states 'Congress shall make no law respecting an establishment of religion, or prohibiting the free exercise thereof.'"

He stood his ground and the IRS let the meter run. Finally, at 8:30 a.m. on February 13, 2001, federal marshals under the direction of a black, born-again marshal named Frank Anderson who should have known better because of his early days being involved in civil rights, seized the church for a six-million dollar IRS tax bill. This was the first time in American history that our government disgraced itself and the Constitution by seizing a Christian church. Pastor Greg A. Dixon (his son), who had replaced his father as active pastor, and many loyal brethren occupied the church 24-hours a day for 92 days. I had the privilege of standing with these brave men and women for a brief period and came away greatly moved by their dedication and determination.

Though the Indianapolis Baptist Temple property is now in receivership, the parishioners have not scattered--they continue meeting at another location in large numbers, and more than a few in the community have accepted Christ, influenced by the courageous stand of Pastor Dixon and his church against the *beast*.

Pastor Dixon, after much research, has put together the following list of 30 ways the IRS tries to control churches in America by threatening to remove their 501(c)(3) exemption from federal tax if they don't conform. For the skeptic, this list was taken from IRS Publication 1828, *Tax Guide for Churches and Other Religious Organizations*, drafted July 26, 1994, IRS

The Making Of A Prophet

Code publications concerning 501(c)(3) *Not-for-Profit Religious Organizations;* two letters from the regional commissioner of the IRS in Cincinnati that were providentially intercepted by the Indianapolis Baptist Temple; twenty-two interrogatories that were included with the letters; and finally, a four-inch thick file that accompanied the letter with news clippings on the church and pastor dating back to 1971. NOTE: When Pastor Dixon refers to "Baptist," he means any independent church.

1. The church must have a "distinct legal existence." According to IRS Publication #557 that legal existence would date from incorporation, page 3. Therefore, a church must be incorporated.

2. The church must admit that it exists by privilege granted by the IRS (tax-exempt) rather than by right granted by God through the Holy scriptures (nontaxable), recognizing another head (state) rather than Christ.

3. The church must have a "recognized creed and form of worship." The IRS must *approve* the creed and form of worship.

4. The church must have a "definite and distinct ecclesiastical government." That is hierarchical (Catholic or Protestant), not Baptist.

5. The church must have a "formal code of doctrine and discipline." Again, this is the Catholic or Protestant model, not Baptist. To Baptists, the Holy scriptures alone are the only rule of faith and practice.

6. The church must have a "distinct religious history." This is denominational (Catholic and Protestant), not Baptist.

7. The church must be an "organization." Again, this is the Catholic and Protestant model, not Baptist.

8. The church must be an "organization of ordained

ministers." Again, Catholic and Protestant, not Baptist. The local Baptist church approves its own ministers who could even be laymen as Charles Haddon Spurgeon and the late G.B. Vick.

9. The church must have these ordained ministers who are "selected after completing prescribed courses of study." Again, Catholic and Protestant, not Baptist. Like the apostles, who had only "been with Jesus," local Baptist churches many times approve pastors who are not educated at all in any formal way.

10. The church must have "established places of worship." True churches many times have no permanent address (place of worship), but because of persecution and other reasons have moved from place to place.

11. The church must submit to the IRS by paying a user fee (tribute) for tax-exempt status. This would be contrary to the scriptures, and US and all state constitutions.

12. The church must be engaged in activities that further "exclusively public purposes rather than private interests." The true Church of Christ exists for the personal and private interests of Christ her Head, not the state.

13. The church must answer to the IRS as to its daily activities.

14. The IRS controls all financial activities of the church including source, donors of $100.00 or more, and expenditures.

15. The church may not use cash or it will be suspected of money laundering. All books and records must be available for IRS inspection at all times.

16. The church must act in the capacity of an informer to the IRS as to who serves at the church in the capacity of pastors, associates, counselors, educational directors, teachers, office help, clerical, and

The Making Of A Prophet

maintenance personnel.

17. The church must inform the IRS as to who the church helps in the area of charity.

18. The church must inform the IRS as to love gifts to evangelists and missionaries over $600.00 by filing a form 1099 on each including those who are regularly supported.

19. The church must use only IRS approved methods of fund raising.

20. The pastor of the church must not preach against the tax system of the US or say anything against the practices and tactics of the IRS.

21. The pastor of the church must answer to the IRS and give unlimited submission to the civil magistrate pertaining to all laws, federal, state and local, including "Public Policy."

22. The pastor of the church must advocate, promote, and actively encourage race mixing if the church has an educational ministry.

23. The pastor of the church cannot influence legislation concerning licensing of church ministries.

24. The pastor of the church cannot engage in political activity opposing pornography.

25. The pastor of the church cannot actively support legislation that declares that children belong to their parents not the state.

26. The pastor of the church cannot actively support legislation opposing a state lottery or other gambling laws.

27. The pastor of the church cannot advocate support of the US or state constitutions as the supreme law of the US or the various states.

28. The pastor of the church cannot oppose the public school system.

29. The pastor of the church cannot declare publicly that the church is to obey God, not government.

30. The pastor of the church cannot oppose laws legalizing sodomy.

Pastor Dixon says in closing:

> In conclusion, may we say that Judge Barker, the IRS, and the Clinton/Reno and Bush/Ashcroft Justice departments may vex the Indianapolis Baptist Temple now but one day she and they will meet the HEAD VEXER. His name is Jesus Christ. The Psalmist David, said speaking of God, "He that sitteth in the heavens shall laugh; the Lord shall have them in derision. Then shall He speak unto them in His wrath, and vex them in His sore displeasure." He then has some words of wisdom for the judges of the earth. "Be wise now therefore, O ye kings: be instructed, ye judges of the earth. Serve the Lord with fear, and rejoice with trembling. Kiss the Son lest He be angry, and ye parish from the way, when His wrath is kindled but a little. Blessed are they that put their trust in Him." (Psalms 2:4,5,10,12)

Now back to the illegality of personal income tax. When I first became interested in this subject I heard about Bill Benson of South Holland, Illinois, who had traveled to all the states in the mid-1980s to research in their archives how each state legislature had ratified the 16th Income Tax Amendment. I contacted him and learned the details. After several months of traveling to 48 states and quite a bit of expense, he returned home fully overwhelmed at what he had discovered. Not one state had properly ratified the amendment. Either they had voted against it, changed the language, or just out-and-out lied. The following entry was recorded on page 487 in Kentucky's journal of the senate, who had ratified the amendment: "...and the question being taken upon the concurring in the adoption of said reso-

The Making Of A Prophet

lution, it was decided in the affirmative. Those who voted in the *affirmative* were:...9. Those who voted in the *negative* were:...22." You read that correctly. But is it a colossal example of bad math or just bureaucratic math--the kind that always adds up to help a bureaucratic agenda? Obviously, in this case it was the latter.

One might ask, why all the devious effort to establish an income tax in 1913? Probably the biggest reason was to cover up the fraudulent Federal Reserve, which is not a government agency. It is a group of 13 major banks who control member banks in the districts.

When our founding fathers wrote the Constitution, they specifically stated in Article One: "Congress shall have the power to coin money and regulate the value thereof." Their intent was that power not be put in the hands of private bankers who could charge enormous amounts of interest, and who could actually then control the country by controlling the money.

For several years after the Constitution was signed, the bankers tried all kinds of tricks to get control. Finally in 1913, on Christmas Eve, Congress with many of its members on vacation, passed the Federal Reserve Act which officially took the power to create money away from the Congress and gave it to private bankers.

The Fed began to print Federal Reserve notes, which cannot be considered constitutional money, because Congress ignored the Constitution in passing this Act.

Some might ask: "What does it matter if Congress or private bankers create the money if it is accepted by the people as a medium of exchange with which to perform business transactions?" What most people don't realize is that this is debt-money, because interest is charged on every dollar created. Let's say that the federal government needs $1 billion to finance a project. The bankers are willing to deliver $1 billion to the government--plus interest, of course. It costs the Federal Reserve about $1,000 to print the $1 billion.

Thousands upon thousands of such transactions have taken place since 1913, so that now, the government is indebted to the bankers for at least $6 trillion, on which the people pay over $400 billion a year in interest alone, with no hope of ever paying off the principal.

And to top that, on this $1 billion that the Federal Reserve received in bonds from this transaction, it is legally allowed to create another $15 billion in new credit to lend to states, municipalities, businesses and individuals. Added to the original $1 billion, they now have $16 billion of credit to give out in loans with their only cost being the $1,000 they spent for printing the original $1 billion lent to the government. Is it a racket? You decide.

Down the line, bankers create money out of nothing, simply by writing numbers in their ledger books, giving interest-laden loans to the American people, allowing them to write checks on their accounts. Using this process, most banks are legally allowed to lend out up to 50 times of what they have on deposit, creating the money out of nothing and then charging interest on it.

The United States has plunged itself terribly into debt since the Federal Reserve Act was passed. In 1910, before its passage, the federal debt was only $1 billion, or $12.40 per citizen. State and local debts were practically nonexistent. By 1920, after only six years of Federal Reserve shenanigans, the federal debt

The Making Of A Prophet

had jumped to $24 billion, or $228 per person.

We could sign over to the bankers all of America, and we would still owe them almost three more Americas. Americans have no idea they have been conquered. They have become tenants and debt-slaves to the bankers. Our children and future generations will be paying the debt forever. We are coming to a point where, eventually, the government will own nothing, the people will own nothing, and the bankers will own everything!

Back in the 1700s, Thomas Jefferson warned the American people that, "If the American people ever allow private banks to control the issue of their money, the banks and corporations will grow to deprive the people of their property, until their children will wake up homeless on the continent their fathers conquered."

It is conquest through the most gigantic fraud and swindle in the history of mankind. And to think that the key to their power and wealth is simply their legal right to create money out of nothing and to lend it out at interest. If they had not been allowed to do that, they could never have gained **secret control of the nation**.

Back in the roaring 20s America had skilled and willing workers, good farmland, a highly efficient transportation system, industries, all that was needed to form a rich nation--all except an adequate supply of money to carry on trade and commerce.

There were other factors involved, but one of the *biggest causes of the depression* was that bankers withheld $8 billion from going into circulation by refusing loans to the population, while at the same time, demanding payment on existing loans, so that money was rapidly taken out of circulation and not replaced.

Because of this control, jobs were waiting to be done, goods were available to be bought, but there was no money. Food was thrown into the ocean while people were starving. Twenty-five percent of the workers were laid off. The banks took possession of hundreds of thousands of farms, homes, and business properties.

When World War II began, our government borrowed huge sums from the banks for military equipment, which put new funds into circulation. People were hired back to work, industries began to blossom, farmers sold their produce, and the economy began to recover. The same bankers, who in the early 30s had no loans for peacetime houses, or food and clothing, suddenly had unlimited billions to lend the government for war purposes. The nation, which a few years earlier could hardly feed its own people, was now producing bombs to send free to the allies.

Just before he died, President Woodrow Wilson is reported to have stated to friends that he had been deceived and had betrayed his country. He was referring to the Federal Reserve Act passed during his presidency.

We know the bankers, the hidden controllers of countries, purposely instigate wars, finance both sides of the same war to frighten people into going billions of dollars into debt for national defense. They have financed Communism, and then turned around and had foreign aid sent to stop the Communism that they financed.

The tens of thousands of young people who are killed, and the hundreds of thousands who are crippled and morally corrupted from war, mean nothing to

The Making Of A Prophet

them. In fact, it doesn't even matter who wins or loses the war, as long as all the countries involved are in debt to them. Many of our politicians have become agents of the bankers, while our two political parties have become their servants. No matter who you elect into high office, Rockefeller and his agents will be running the government behind the scenes--you can be sure of it. How else could something so diabolical as the Federal Reserve, something so destructive to the national interest of the people, be allowed to continue so long? They accomplished it by controlling all of the news media and information centers, by controlling the purse strings--to prevent the people from learning the truth. They blame the people for causing the increase in debt and the inflation of prices, when they know that the real cause is the debt-money system itself.

Very few people know that the United States has been in a state of bankruptcy since 1933. Franklin D. Roosevelt, under the "War Powers" Act, committed high-treason against every American by signing the Emergency Banking Act which declared the country bankrupt and insolvent, placing the government into the hands of the bankers as receivers. And that meant that Common Law juries of the Constitution could be replaced with Homage and Advisory juries; the courts would become Admiralty courts, which is why judges refuse to listen to a patriot who bases his defense on the Constitution. What this means is that the United States is really governed by the Secretary of the Treasury, who is also governor of the International Monetary Fund.

The IRS, FBI, CIA, ATF, and other agencies, report to that office, as do all US military forces, state governors, etc. The IRS is nothing more than a private collection agency for the Federal Reserve. They put on their letterheads, "Department of Treasury" wanting people to think they're the Treasury Department of the US when they're the Treasury Department of the Federal Reserve.

Those close to President Kennedy say that he was getting ready to repeal the Emergency Banking Act and reinstate the gold and silver standard which would solve this nation's indebtedness. With the same stroke of a pen he was also going to become the second president, after Andrew Jackson, to destroy the credit checkbook money debt system and put the bankers and compromised public officials up on charges of high crimes under the Law of Nations. On June 4, 1963, he signed Executive Order 11110 to print US dollars with no debt or interest attached, bypassing the Federal Reserve. Five months later he was assassinated. Immediately upon his death, the printing ceased and the currency was withdrawn.

This system which puts the credit of the nations into the hands of the Federal Reserve follows the 5th plank of the Communist Manifesto which demands: "Centralization of credit in the hands of the state, by means of a national bank with state capital and an exclusive monopoly."

It is painfully obvious that one major reason the IRS exists is people control. Remember Revelation 13? The Antichrist causes everyone to take a mark on his body before they can buy or sell. His *beast* government will need complete control of all the people to accomplish this. And the personal information naive Americans so carelessly fill out on their income tax forms does just

The Making Of A Prophet

that.

Some might ask, "Is there nothing to be done then?" My answer is, you must let God be your guide as to the road you are to travel. Many, many participants in the tax rebellion movement are born-again Christians.

One obvious action to make America healthy again is to put pressure on the government to repeal the Federal Reserve Act of 1913 and demand that Congress again be allowed to create and control the money of the nation. Only government banks, under the supervision of the peoples' representatives, would issue and control all money and credit. A $60,000 loan made to build a house would require only $60,000.00 in repayment, with a minor fee, not $255,931.00, as it is now. Everyone who supplied materials and labor to build the house would get paid just as they are today, but the bankers would not get $195,931.00 in usury.

A debt-free America would mean that mothers would not have to work, but could remain home with their children. Juvenile delinquency would decrease rapidly. The elimination of the usury and debt would be the equivalent of a 50% rise in the purchasing power of every worker. The bankers would no longer be able to steal billions of dollars from the people every year in interest. America would once again become the envy of the world, being prosperous and powerful beyond the wildest dreams of its citizens. Anything is possible with prayer backed up with action. Write editorials in your local newspapers. Write to your congressmen and get others to write. Do your own research to determine if *you* are paying an unlawful personal income tax.

You might ask, "But how will the government operate if people stopped paying income tax?" The truth is, a very large percentage of income tax goes to pay the interest on the national debt created by ungodly bankers (usury). There is never any hope of paying the trillions of national debt--Americans have become slaves of the private bankers.

Billions of your tax money goes to foreign aid, another example of Congress violating the Constitution. More billions help finance a bankrupt Social Security program. If citizens invested in conservative retirement plans rather than pay social security, they would be much further ahead financially. Few Americans realize the personal income tax is voluntary. Author Charles Weisman explains it quite expertly:

> Since there is no section on the IR Code that makes you liable for income taxes, when you file a tax return, YOU are the one assessing yourself, and you swear "under penalties of perjury" that YOU are the one who owes the tax. This is what the IRS wants since their Code actually says that the Secretary of Treasury is responsible for assessing the taxes owed, as stated in Section 6203 of the code.
>
> This makes it clear that you have to get an assessment (a bill) for your tax before you are liable for it, just as you would with your property tax. Yet the IRS continues with their deceptive claim that you must assess yourself. What they want is your *signature* on their tax form which is your consent to pay their taxes.
>
> ...If we are not required to file a tax return, then what is our obligation to it? If it is **not required** then it is **voluntary**, which means you have no legal obligation. The IRC was written to **deceive**, **confuse**, and **mislead** the American people and make it appear that you have to **pay these taxes**. Since there is no lawful requirement, you are merely obliging their request for

The Making Of A Prophet

your wages and you voluntarily give it to them. This point of a voluntary payment of income taxes was expressed by the US Supreme Court in: *US V. Flora,* 362 US 145, when it stated: *"Our system of taxation is based upon voluntary assessment and payment, not upon distraint* (force).*"*

The IRS has also stated that the income tax is voluntary: *"The IRS's primary task is to collect taxes under a VOLUNTARY compliance system." (1980 Internal Revenue Report,* Jerome Kurtz, Commissioner)

From the Internal Revenue Manual, 1975: *"Our tax system is based on self assessment and VOLUNTARY compliance."*

Thus, the IRS has the authority to encourage you to voluntarily comply--they have *No Other Authority*.

Why is the income tax voluntary? It must be voluntary because compulsory payment of taxes on wages would violate many rights and provisions of the Constitution. Remember, the income tax is an excise tax (as expressed by the Supreme Court in the *Brushaber* case) but is assessed and collected as a direct tax. If the government forced, or required you to pay a direct tax it would be contrary to the apportionment clause of the Constitution, so it must be voluntary. The IRS knows this and this is why it uses the clever and misleading statements in the IRC that actually say it is voluntary but appears as though it is not.

...When **you voluntarily sign and submit a 1040 Form** you waive your rights and agree to be bound to any rules and regulations of the IRS that did not apply to you before you signed. You now have waived your 4th and 5th Amendment Rights to retain personal information and records which could be used as evidence against you in any court or criminal case. The 4th and 5th Amendments absolutely guarantee every American the right to keep his personal papers private, and the right of refusing to give evidence against himself. But, when you sign and submit a 1040 tax return you are now vulnerable to IRS prosecution.

This becomes further proof that you are not required to sign and file a 1040 tax form. Because, if you were, that requirement (to sign under oath) would be unconstitutional, as it would violate your 5th Amendment right, not to be compelled to be a witness against yourself. The US Supreme Court (in *Garner v. United States*, 424 US 648, 1976) has upheld the right to claim and exercise the 5th Amendment Constitutional RIGHT against self-incrimination on a tax return. It stated that:
"The information revealed in the preparation and filing of an income tax return is, for the 5th Amendment analysis, the testimony of a witness as that term is used herein."

When you sign (under penalty of perjury) and file a tax return you are waiving many of your constitutional rights, including the 1st, 4th, 5th, 7th, and 9th Amendments. By so doing, you are now giving the IRS jurisdiction over you. If you make even the slightest mistake (e.g.--being off by ten cents) you can be tried for "code violations" and be put in prison. This is because the Uniform Commercial Code, which took place over our Common Law, allows the IRS to operate under private contract. Thus, Americans should be terrified to even think of signing and filing a tax return. When you do sign and file a tax return, you have changed your legal status from a citizen and freeman to a taxpayer and regulated slave.

So the basis of the IRS and its Code is a **voluntary** tax that is made to appear as a mandatory law; which means that 95% of the practices of the IRS are based on fraud, lies, deception, extortion, blackmail and sheer bluff. These immoral acts of lies and deception are not the end of the worst of what the IRS has done

The Making Of A Prophet

to exact wages from the American people. Other immoral and unlawful acts that IRS agents have admitted to (in Congressional hearings) are:

-- Robs money from bank accounts (without court orders)

-- Forces employers to withhold taxes with no pay in return (involuntary servitude)

-- Robs from paychecks (deductions without court orders)

-- Liens property (without court order)

-- Hires prostitutes to entrap men or get information from them

-- Holds spurious (false) proceedings with agents acting as judges (tax court) assessing outrageous taxes without proof

-- Holds people hostage (in jail) and conspires against their rights

-- Seizes and sells homes, autos and other property without trial by jury (violation of 7th Amendment rights) or a court order

If these last words from author Weisman don't start your blood boiling and motivate you to action, then you are either brain dead or you are one of many chicken-livered Americans who would continue to be slaves rather than risk retaliation from the *beast*. When that day comes when the *beast* orders you to go down to the post office to receive a mark, the bio ID chip, you'll be first in line. God help you!

TOP & BOTTOM: Indiana Baptist Temple during a 92-day siege. The first time in American history the government disgraced itself and the Constitution by seizing a church for taxes.

SIXTEEN

WE HAVE ALMOST COME TO THE END of our journey. I trust it wasn't too rough going for you. I know my comments about organized religion, education, and government may seem harsh and impossible to embrace. I just ask that you not draw any hasty conclusions. Someday much of it may make sense.

I know there are many fine Christians serving in organizations that do bare fruit. But it is my sense that they are God's Plan B, not His Plan A. His Plan A, in my thinking, has always been the local church operating as in the New Testament, with plurality of leadership, the five-fold ministries, the spiritual gifts flourishing with much emphasis on evangelism, and making disciples to Christ rather than to church membership. A New Testament-type body meeting is a hospital to have one's wounds bound up for the next day's battle, not an exclusive country club where the best music groups and preachers are "hired" with love offerings to tickle ears and raise attendance. Sunday school and church lectures are poor substitutes for the father's role as spiritual teacher of God's truths.

Soon we will see a great upheaval of all the idols Americans hold so dear--technology, the stock market, personal savings, careers, new cars, sports. Everything and anything not bolted down with Holy Spirit nuts and bolts will be shaken and destroyed.

Prophet Dumitru Duduman in his 1992 book, *Through The Fire*, reported a vision he had of our coastal cities under nuclear bomb attack. When he wrote that, most people were highly skeptical that this could ever happen to America. But after the Trade Center buildings were destroyed, many of these scoffers have had to reprogram their thinking.

God will allow these events to occur because we have ignored the things that matter to Him for a long time. We forbade any reference to Him in our schools and public places; we passed laws protecting homosexuality and sex training to the very young. And when young girls became pregnant, we made it legal for them to murder their unborn babies, **50 MILLION OF THEM** since Roe vs. Wade.

As the increase in a woman's birth pains signals the closeness of a new birth, so the increase in crises and disasters signals the closeness of Christ's second coming and the birth of His new kingdom.

Eight hundred years before Jesus, the prophet Joel described the last days in more detail, "Alas for the day! For the day of the Lord is at hand, and as a destruction from the Almighty shall it come. Our food will disappear before our eyes; all joy and gladness will be ended in the temple of our God. The seed rots in the ground; barns and granaries are empty; the grain has dried up in the fields. The cattle groan with hunger; the herds stand perplexed for there is no pasture for them; the sheep bleat in misery. Lord, help us! For the heat has withered the pastures and burned up all the trees.

The Making Of A Prophet

Even the wild animals cry to you for help, for there is not water for them. The creeks are dry and the pastures are scorched." (Joel 1:15-20)

The world economy is not controlled by man's intellect or his stupidity--but by a raindrop. Without rain, crops don't grow, with too much rain they can't be planted. Without rain you can't have chickens, eggs, meat, or bread. God used the rain, or lack of it (famine), as a judgment tool in the Old Testament many times. He has promised never again to destroy the world by water, but he will use "natural disasters" to get the attention of America and the world before the final fire storm begins.

This has been confirmed by many prophets from yesteryear up to the present. Perhaps the most graphic comes from Dumitru Duduman whom I mentioned earlier. He was a Romanian who was tortured repeatedly by the Communists for smuggling Bibles. While in his cell the angel Gabriel appeared and told him that he would go to America. The following are parts of his testimony from his book, *Through The Fire*.

> ...it was late at night...a light surrounded me. Out of the light I heard the same voice. (That was with me in jail and in my house in Italy) "Dumitru, why are you so despaired?"
>
> I said, "Why did you punish me? What did I do that was so rotten that you brought me to the United States? I have nowhere to lie my head down. I can't understand anybody."
>
> He said, "Dumitru, didn't I tell you that I am here with you also? I brought you here to this country because this country will burn."
>
> "Then why did you bring me here to burn? Why didn't you let me die in my own country?"

"Dumitru, have patience and I will tell you. Get beside me."

I don't know what it was, brothers. I got beside the angel. He showed me all of California. He showed me all the cities of California. Then he showed me Las Vegas.

"You see what I have shown you. This is Sodom and Gomorrah. In one day it will burn. "He said, "It's sin has reached the Holy One. "He showed me another great city. "Do you know what city this is?"

I said, "No."

He said, "This is New York City. This is Sodom and Gomorrah. In one day it will burn. "He showed me Florida. He said, "This is Florida. This is Sodom and Gomorrah. In one day it will burn."

He didn't let me say a word until he brought me back to the place we had left. He said, "Now Dumitru. You can talk to me." He said, "I brought you to this country. Dumitru, I want to wake up a lot of people. I love this country. I love the people. I want to save them. America will burn."

And I said, "How can I save them? I can't even speak their language. Who knows me here? How will they call me?"

He said, "Don't worry. I will be ahead of you. I will make great healings amongst the American people. You will go to television stations, radio stations, and churches. Tell them everything I tell you. Don't hide anything. If you try to hide anything, I will punish you. America will burn."

"How will America burn? It is so powerful."

He said, "The Russian spies have discovered where the most powerful nuclear missiles are in America. It will start with an internal revolution in America started by the Communists. Afterwards when Americans think there is peace and quiet and everything is all right,

The Making Of A Prophet

from the oceans, from Russia, Cuba, Nicaragua, Central America, Mexico, will come an attack. The Russians will bombard the nuclear missile silos in America. America will burn."

I said, "What will you do with the Church?"

He said, "The Church has left me."

I said, "How? Don't you have people here?"

He said, "People honor people. The honor that should be given to God, they give to other people. Americans think highly of themselves. In the Church there is divorce. In the Church there is adultery, and fornication. In the Church there is sodomy. In the Church there is abortion, and all kinds of sin. Jesus Christ doesn't live in sin. He lives in HOLINESS. I brought you here so you could cry out loud. Don't be afraid. I am with you. Tell them to stop sinning. God never stops forgiving. Tell them to repent. He will forgive them. Tell them to start preparing themselves so I can save them in the day of trouble."

I said, "How will you save the Church if America will burn?"

He said, "Tell them as I tell you. As I saved the three young men from the oven of fire, and Daniel from the mouth of the lion, that is how I will save them. Tell them to stop sinning and repent. Israel doesn't recognize the Messiah, they place their trust in the power of the Jews in America. When God will hit America all the nations will be terrified. God will raise up China, Japan, and many other nations and they will beat the Russians. They will push them back to the gates of Paris. There they will make a peace treaty, but they will make the Russians their leader. All the nations with the Russians as their leader, go against Israel. It's not that they want to. God makes them. Israel won't have the help of the Jews in America anymore. In their terror, when they see what is coming, they will call upon the Messiah. The Messiah will come to help Israel. Then the Church of God will meet him in the clouds." (I Thessalonians 4:16)

I said, "If you are the angel of God, everything you tell me has to be written in the Bible. If it is not, then I can't tell the Americans."

"Tell them to read Jeremiah 51:8-15, he names it THE MYSTERY BABYLON, THE GREAT ADULTERESS. Also, Revelation 18, the whole chapter. There it says clearly what will happen to America."

"Why did he name it THE MYSTERY BABYLON?"

"Tell them because all the nations of the world immigrated into America, and America accepted them. America accepted Buddha, the Devil church, the Sodomite church, the Mormon church, and all kinds of wickedness. America was a Christian nation. Instead of stopping them, they went after their gods. Because of this, he named them THE MYSTERY BABYLON.

I must point out that our Constitution guarantees the right for immigrants to worship as they choose but that doesn't mean that I, as a Christian, should accept their religion or give them special privileges. In the world there will always be religions and philosophies competing with Christianity. But the Lord says, "Come out from among them and be ye separate."

Dumitru later stated on August 10, 1991, that the angel came and told him more things would soon happen.

-- War with Saddam Hussein would restart.
-- Nuclear weapons would be used.
-- Saddam will go against Israel.
-- The United States will be involved.

The Making Of A Prophet

Armageddon is just on the horizon, the greatest battle ever fought by the armies of the whole world gathered together in the valley of Jesreel (Megiddo), about 50 miles north of Jerusalem. This is what John wrote in Revelation 19 of the Bible.

"...and I saw the *beast* and the kings of the earth, and their armies, gathered together to make war against Him (Jesus Christ) that sat on the horse and against His army. And the *beast* (world ruler) that wrought miracles before him, with which he deceived them that had received the mark of the *beast* (a mark in your right hand or forehead) and them that worshipped his image; these both were cast alive into a lake of fire burning with brimstone..."

Hollywood fantasy stuff? Afraid not. It will happen because the Bible says it will. Every single prophesy of the Bible from before Jesus Christ till the present time has been proven true, regardless of what the world's intelligentsia would have you believe.

For instance, the prophet Ezekiel foretold over 2500 years ago that Israel would be scattered all over the world because of their iniquities, but in the last days they would regather in Palestine. We all know that Jews have been returning to Palestine, especially during the last 30 years, and that in 1948 they again became a nation.

The prophet Daniel, about 555 BC, prophesied the destruction of the all powerful Babylon, then foretold the Medo-Persian Empire rise and fall, the downfall of the Grecian Empire under Alexander the Great, and then the rise of the old Roman Empire. He prophesied that just before the return of Jesus Christ, ten nations would evolve out of the old Roman Empire before the rise of a world ruler. Today that federation is called the European Union. He also said that in the last days, "Many shall run to and fro...chariots (automobiles) raging in the streets...they shall seem like torches, they shall run like lightning."

Current Mideastern conflicts will be resolved by a seven year peace treaty that will be spear-headed by a charismatic leader the Bible refers to as the Antichrist. This world leader will become head of the European Union. This seven-year peace treaty will include Israel and her neighbors, and the Antichrist will permit Israel to rebuild their temple, but when it is finished, he will sit in it and declare himself to be the savior of the world. He will perform miracles that will deceive millions--many of whom will be lukewarm Christians. He will break the peace treaty at the end of three-and-one-half years and make war on Christians and Jews. The US government will merge into the global *beast* government.

The Antichrist, who most prophets would agree is alive today, must have an accomplice if he is to control people--you guessed it right-- the almighty computer. You are already in the master file of L.U.C.I.D., a global control system of linked data bases, an electronic straitjacket, if you will, that allows the tracking of every man, woman, and child on planet earth. L.U.C.I.D. is a brainchild of our National Security Agency.

A growing number of the true bride of Christ are now realizing their personal computer puts their personal lives right into the *beast* government's spotlight. Remember, WWW stands for World Wide *Web* and in the Hebrew alpha-numeric code translates into 666, the mark of the Antichrist. It all began with the

The Making Of A Prophet

numbering system of Social Security. Then came the credit cards and soon, the national I.D. MARC card. Very convenient, but along with IRS tax forms people innocently fill out, the objective is the same--people control. Since plastic cards can be broken, stolen or lost, a wonderful new innovation will be offered. A number can be invisibly laser-tattooed on your forehead or back of the hand, or an implant--a biochip smaller than a grain of rice, can be put on your body painlessly, cosmetically acceptable, that can store megabytes of vital information. Chips are already being used to control wildlife, pets, and segments of the military. But be forewarned! According to Revelation 14:9, all who take the Antichrist's mark in order to buy and sell freely, will ultimately lose their souls. All who refuse it will be executed by the *beast* government since they will be considered a destabilizing force in society. Again, scoffers need to be reminded that not one of the Bible's many prophecies has ever been proven wrong!

Will these events occur in your lifetime? They've already started; the ongoing Mideastern crisis is the beginning of the end. The last great event? Listen carefully for it involves you personally. Most people are interested in what is going to happen to them after death; this is the Bible's answer:

"And I saw a great white throne, and him that sat on it, from whose face the earth and the heaven fled away; and there was found no place for them. And I saw the dead, small and great, stand before God; and those things which were written in the books, according to their works. And death and hell were cast into the lake of fire, this is the second death. And whosoever was not found in the book of life was cast into the lake of fire." (Revelation 20:10-15) Is your name in the book? Most people's names are not. Even that was prophesied by Jesus, Himself. "...but the gate is small and the way is narrow that leads to life and few are those who find it." (Matthew 7:13)

Don't be fooled into thinking that your future is predestined. God didn't make Adam a robot, He gave him a will, the freedom to love Him or rebel against Him and His commandments. And the greatest commandment of all was that Jesus Christ would become the savior of the world, not as an insurance policy for all mankind, but for the individuals who saw themselves in need of forgiveness for the wrongs of their lives and would accept Jesus Christ as God's plan for them to be reconciled to Him. Have you done this? If not, your name is not in the book.

If you're a Christian, don't fall for the dribble that you'll be raptured before the great tribulation begins. Those who believe that haven't a clue that God has, and is, warning them through the prophets to prepare spiritually and physically. Their lack of discernment is caused by years of their not being sensitive to God's voice in their lives and, have instead, listened to false prophets--their pastors. The truth, that God did not build the ark for Noah, totally escapes them.

I have determined that my "guide" to survival for hard times ahead is going to be the Holy Spirit. In addition, I would offer these suggestions to those who have taken this book seriously:

1. Ground your faith in God and His Word, not in man, meetings, or circumstance. Faith cometh by hearing--hearing His voice daily through the Bible--and your spirit obeying Him, learning to trust Him in the

The Making Of A Prophet

little things so you'll be able to trust Him in the big things when the world around you is panic stricken. Learn to claim His promises. There are 7,000 of them. For instance, Psalm 37:18-19 says, "The Lord knows the days of the upright, and their inheritance shall be forever. They shall not be ashamed in the evil time, and in the days of famine they shall be satisfied."

2. "Don't lay up treasures on earth (stocks, bonds, large insurance policies, retirement plans, investments for the future) where moth and rust corrupts (the investments will become riskier each year)... for where your treasure is, there will be your heart also." (Matthew 6:19) "Lay up for yourselves treasures in heaven by giving to God's work, feeding the starving, supporting those who can show good fruit, etc."

3. Learn now how to relate to your brothers and sisters in Christ. Don't just visit with them in meetings but look for ways to serve them during the week. The strong church in hard times will be one in spirit, meeting each other's needs. Communal living may prove to be a not too radical idea at that--especially when brothers will not be able to make their own mortgage payments, or even taxes.

4. Learn now how to feed your family nutritionally. Learn how to grow your own food and the physical and spiritual benefits of fasting one day a week.

Just before Christ returns, He will give His bride (that's you, if you truly love Him) tremendous signs and wonders to help reach the lost in your community, and you'll be more effective than Christians have ever been before in history. That "dunamis" power the early Church had will be a firecracker compared to the Holy Spirit bomb blast needed to smash intensified forces from hell that will be unleashed on the world.

So let's not stop with what we read in Acts or Corinthians. God never stands still. He will guide the way over new horizons if we will only keep seeking His will and not relax back into our comfortable traditional ruts. Remember the definition of a rut (a grave with the ends kicked out)? That pretty much sums up what I'm saying in this book.

A lot of Christians are stuck fast in their ruts and won't go out on that limb of faith. Wherever you are with God, don't stop believing Him for more today than you did yesterday. If He has given you a tough ministry, He'll give you rest periods, but don't let vacation become a way of life. If you're an older Christian, don't kid yourself into thinking that because you're "religious" outwardly, you're still actively seeking God, because probably you're not. And you young people, don't let the religionists try to convert you to their traditions. Instead, accept Jesus Christ in all His fullness--then go out and be a free person.

As you travel along on your faith journey, if you find the path getting narrower and more difficult, don't give up. You may be criticized severely by the "religionists" for not walking to their beat. Don't be too hard on them for not hearing the same beat, but try to show them how they can improve their hearing.

When you really get close to the cross and begin to feel the pain of the nails, don't shrink back, it's for a purpose in your life, and it won't last forever. Suffering can wreck or sweeten you--the choice is yours.

END

Epilogue

If the economy collapses, or some other catastrophic event throws the country into chaos, an enemy might execute HEMP, a high altitude, electromagnetic burst, or set of nuke bursts, that will destroy every electrical device's electronic solid-state circuitry within line of sight. It will not physically hurt flesh. It could come from a submarine and would take eight-to-ten minutes to accomplish. Subsequently, all electronics with solid-state components will shut down--no cars running, no electricity, no phones, no communications. Cars 25-years old may run, and many battery-powered radios may also make it through, especially if shielded in a metal container.

If you see a big flash that you suspect is an attack, drop flat on the ground, count slowly to 200. If nothing happens, get up and head for shelter. If it's a high altitude bright flash you'll have about 15-20 minutes to get into your shelter.

Do not mistake HEMP for a low altitude, aerial burst nuclear detonation with a big cloud, called a nudet. In the event you are in one of the safe areas, you may not see a HEMP burst. But if suddenly the electricity goes off and you don't hear any radio stations, you can figure the attack is on. If you can't tell a HEMP burst from a low altitude burst, get to cover as fast as you can. If there is no blast and heat immediately after the flash, then you know it was a HEMP burst.

An enemy may use neutron warheads called clean bombs, with little collateral damage in the ensuing nuclear lay down, to kill flesh, not crops, because he needs our resources. Distance, mass, and time are your friends in a nuclear attack. If you're prepared, you will have a good chance of survival if you're not too close to target cities, on the east side near the target, or down wind. The prevailing winds over the U.S. are west to east; fallout will be worst on the east side of any given target. If you're within 12 miles of a one-megaton blast, your survival chances are slim. Soviet MIRVs are suspected to have ten one-megaton warheads. More damage can be caused that way than with one ten-megaton warhead. High winds will go out to over 25 miles in all directions. But if you're more than 25 miles west, you won't be much affected by fallout from that particular hit.

Don't look at the fireball. You'll be blinded. However, if you're within 100-400 miles of another nudet west of you, you'll be in trouble. If you're closer than that, you'll have some chance of survival, but you'll have to have made extensive preparations and have moved fast.

Gamma rays travel on line of sight from the nudet like rifle bullets. Alpha and Beta radiation are in the fallout, but will deteriorate within weeks. The fallout dust must be kept away from you. Get some dirt in bags for mass, or bags of corn or wheat, second-best idea, over and around your shelter. If anyone goes out of the shelter, his outer clothes must be left outside the house. If possible, don't send the same person out twice. Alternate exposure, and only for short periods.

You have to be prepared. People running around looking for food, or looting, etc., will be dead in one-to-three weeks, even sooner if closer to the nudet. Under no circumstances do you go outside during the first two or three days. Pre-positioning the required items in the shelter is the ticket through this.

Your first need will be water, at least a month's

supply. You must have containers. Plastic milk jugs or Pepsi type two-liter bottles will work and are handy in a shelter, but glass containers are better for the long haul because of some plastic contamination. You're going to need at least a gallon of water a day for every person, especially if there is vomiting, because it will be needed to flush the body of irradiated particles.

Take two teaspoons of baking soda and four of salt, and four or five of sugar or honey in a gallon of water during the days you are vomiting up precious body electrolytes, due to poisoning. Plain liquids won't do it. Gatorade will work, but it's expensive.

Any water exposed to fallout dust must be filtered. Other than well or spring water, all other water must be purified. Clorox will do nothing against radioactive particles. You can make a simple water filter out of a metal bucket, sand, straw, stones, and dirt, or go out and purchase one now. There are 60 gallons of water in the hot water tank of most homes. Have some hose handy, and that's a swell place to build your shelter, next to the water tank.

A hand pump can be installed on most wells with a fitting that allows pumping water through a hose directly to the house. You can get a local plumber to put a hand pump on your well along with your present submersible pump. Lehman Brothers Hardware, Box 41, Kidron, Ohio 44636 (216) 857-5441-5771 has a catalog with hundreds of water-handling items, as well as non-electric aids.

If you have a year-round spring you're okay. But after the fallout, and the rain has cleansed the land, you'll still need clean water. One teaspoon of Clorox in ten gallons will purify, but a better purifier is food-grade hydrogen peroxide. Ten drops of 35 percent food grade per gallon will take care of every strain of bad bacteria. A health food store can order it for you.

If you have a four-inch or larger diameter casing in your well, you can use a tubular well bucket available for $33 from Lehman's. You drop it into the casing with a rope, the valve opens, water flows in and you have two to three gallons of water. If you're smart, you can make one out of PVC pipe with a caged rubber ball for a valve in the bottom. You may have to pull the existing plumbing from the well casing to get your tubular bucket down. That usually takes a three-to-four foot "T" handle, made out of pipe, with a 1⅛-inch or 1¼-inch thread on the end. A plumber can make it. But see him now, forget him later.

You can figure how much food you're going to need for at least one-to-four weeks. Remember, you must stay in your shelter for at least one week. If you're closer to the blast, maybe four-to-five weeks. Pray for rain to wash away the radioactive dust.

You must have some critical food-support items. Vitamin and mineral pills will help. Don't take aspirin because it will hurt your tender stomach lining if you've been irradiated. Use Tylenol. You need calcium citrate, at least 100 mg a day, to fight off nuclear effects on bone marrow. Adults need to take five drops of Lugols Solution (potassium iodide) daily, children, two drops daily for 100 days after the fallout begins, for protection against radiation. Iodide pills are handier and readily available. Vitamins C, D, and B3 should be taken also.

If possible don't use candles or kerosene lamps in the shelter; they will use up your oxygen. Blue lips mean not enough air, fan some in somehow. Have flashlights and extra batteries ready. Get some boxes so you can keep everyone's stuff separate. Canned goods are great, but you must have a can opener.

Forget about your freezer because you won't have electricity. Dehydrated survival packages are okay, but expensive. Grains and lentils are your best bet--wheat, barley, rolled oats, beans and rice. Store them in plastic milk bottles or five-gallon buckets. Get a hand grinder, now. Don't forget honey or sugar. Get boxes of powdered milk; it will keep two or three years.

Today, you can get 100 pounds of shelled corn for eight dollars at the local farmers co-op. You soak it overnight, or until it gets soft; boiling works quicker. Then put brown sugar on it. Ten pounds of dry corn will swell to about 25 pounds of food. The same goes for other grain which you can buy from local farmers.

You'll need iodized salt, baking powder, etc. If your spouse won't cooperate with you now, don't worry about it. Work alone. He or she will sure cooperate with you when the bomb goes off, I guarantee it. If you can find a wholesale grocer, you can get your foodstuffs in cases--makes it easier to handle.

Wood is going to be the resource of choice for fuel. Coal keeps well, but you must use a cast iron grate in your stove to avoid ruining it because coal will melt steel grates and stove bottoms. It also must be kept dry, but it won't rot like wet wood.

Saving old motor oil to use in starting fires is an idea, and besides, the EPA will have been blasted out of existence anyway. You can burn it in a pinch, but be careful, it'll put out fumes, especially if you do not have an airtight stove or your stovepipes are in poor condition.

Heating water can be a problem unless you think ahead. You must have a lid on the water pot to heat it quickly and economically. Cast iron stuff is going to be the rage. Carbon steel knives stay sharp longer than stainless. How about a meat saw? You must have food-support items. What about matches or a magnifying glass to start a fire? Buy a whole case of matches for bartering. Plumbers' candles come singly or order them special, 200 to a box, from a hardware store. Keep them in a cool place, they melt.

Your dollars are going to be changed into a new currency soon. Spend your dollars for these goods now. When money becomes almost useless, you'll have valuable items to barter with.

Get a painter's dust mask (or two) for everyone in the shelter so that when you go outside you won't be breathing fallout dust. Have a bucket and plastic bags to handle human waste. If you have a basement shelter, you might cut a hole in the septic down pipe and fix something up to allow pouring urine into it, but nothing else, unless you have plenty of water to flush it down. Cover each deposit in the bucket with newspaper shreds, or have a bag of lime handy.

Toilet paper and coffee will be the rage in trade goods. Have flashlights and batteries; it's going to be dark in that shelter without them. Female necessities should not be forgotten. Keep clean with baby wipes, a box or two for each person.

Get yourself a shortwave radio with plenty of extra batteries, and store it in an ammo box or an old stove or refrigerator. A ham transceiver or CB radio hooked up to a car battery will allow you to communicate with others. What about firearms? Depending on your convictions, you may need them to defend against rioters who will die in a few days from radiation exposure.

Here are some ideas for survival over a longer period of time. Fifty-five gallon oil drums can be obtained, usually free, from tractor service dealers, service stations, etc. You can buy a 55-gallon, drum-attachable rotary pump for your oil and gas from many sources for about $70. Gasoline spoils, depending on octane rating (get 87), in a year or so unless you treat it with "Sta-bil," manufactured by Gold Eagle company in Chicago. You can extend its life by about a year. The house that China built, Wal-Mart, should have it.

Remember, most modern engines have solid state ignitions and will be destroyed in the HEMP attack unless it's in a root cellar, or buried, or below the line of sight of the bursts.

A generator will be handy, and also a chain saw, but do not depend on gas-powered equipment for the long haul because gasoline may not be available. Bring any 12-volt storage batteries into the house in the winter. If they are not fully charged, they will freeze up and be worthless in the spring. There'll be none for sale during "silent spring."

Get some rope, tape, string, and some aluminum metal rolls and sheeting. It'll come in handy as will silicone caulking. Lots of wire is a must. Generators and chain saws need oil, too. Think. Get extra chains for the chain saw and have crosscut saws and axes to manually cut firewood. Get all your hand tools sharpened. Get a hacksaw. A brace and bit will be useful. Go to farm auction sales and get tools cheap. Get a hand grinder from Lehman Brothers to sharpen your tools and a whetstone to sharpen your knives.

As for gardening concerns: you can get hermetically-sealed seeds in cans from Walton Seeds at 1-800-847-0465. They sell for about $16 each. There are enough seeds, in foil packets, to plant a basketball-court-sized garden. They'll keep for years. The Walton seeds, except for the corn, are non-hybrid. Seeds saved from matured plants this year, grown from hybrid seeds, usually will not produce much, if anything, the next year. America has trapped herself with hybrids.

Your rototiller probably won't work after the HEMP attack. If it does, great. If not, you'll have to use a spade or hand plow. Fertilizer will keep forever, and in bags, can be used as mass around your shelter. Insecticide is another consideration. Put it in a sock and dust the plants (by tapping the sock). Canning is great, but you'll need equipment. Get it now. Buy small and wide-mouth jars and lids. If you have extra money, get a bunch. You can barter those too.

As for a shelter, you can build one out of plywood in one corner of your basement if you don't have a root cellar. Second best are plastic sheets, two or three layers hung from the rafters as a tent. Seal any basement windows and doors with duct tape or foam spray if time permits. Any windows near the shelter should also be blocked with any solid material available.

What about sleeping? You might not have any heat, so think. If you use two-by-fours as studs for your shelter, you can easily make flat sleeping bunks and hang them from overhead. Cut them 24-inches by six feet. Get some air mattresses.

Even without a nuclear attack, there is a strong possibility that in an economic collapse, you're going to have to have this kind of survival stuff anyhow. But if there is an attack, you'll live a lot longer than the folks whose first thoughts of preparation will be when they see the flash. They'll only have 20 minutes at best. Worst case, they'll only have 20 seconds. You can be in your shelter in 20 seconds.

All this will sound too extreme to many, and it is. But the thinking person knows deep down that something is wrong in this old world. Evil is on a rampage, God and His Commandments are made light of, and what seemed secure a few years back can no longer be counted on. A catastrophic occurrence suddenly seems believable. Survival will be the all-consuming motivation in the near future and much of it will be very extreme.

An expert in extreme survival techniques is Rick Asher, the Special Forces guy who helped me with the sniper details in *Let The Games Begin*.

When the bomb went off in The World Trade Center basement in 1994, Rick's brother, Vincent, was a VIP working on the 106th floor. Rick, because of his training and smartness, immediately had a survival plan for his brother. When they next met, he handed him his .45 automatic and said, "Take this piece, hide it in a secure place and keep it loaded. Here's an ad from a company that supplies sport parachutes. These chutes are small and pack down to a compact bundle. Get one and stow it in your office too. If your co-workers find out you'll take a lot of ribbing, and you might be forced to remove the .45. So keep your mouth shut.

"But here's the program. If a bombing or fire occurs and you're in danger of not getting down safely, blow out the window behind your desk with the .45, throw on the chute, and go through the window." Vincent accepted the .45 but he never bought the sport chute. Rick could tell his brother was just humoring him. As fate would have it, Vincent never had to follow the plan--he was transferred some months before 9-11 occurred.

Extreme survival preparation will always be ridiculed by those uninformed or in denial of possible danger around them. I wonder how many of those who were forced to jump out the windows of the Twin Towers on 9-11 would have ridiculed Rick's plan of survival prior to the disaster? Incidentally, Rick's brother is now all ears whenever Rick starts talking about preparing for what is about to happen in America.

Acknowledgements

The author wishes to thank the following persons for providing certain critical information included in this book.

>Richard Jolly
>Dr. Greg A. Dixon
>Walter DuMont
>Charles Weisman
>Cecil J. DuCille
>Rick Asher
>Dumitru Duduman
>Dr. Bill Hamon
>Texe Marrs